Stephen Grimer
OP

Duel in the Shadows

DUEL
IN THE
SHADOWS

TRUE ACCOUNTS OF ANTI-NAZI
UNDERGROUND WARFARE
DURING WORLD WAR II

Written and Illustrated by

ALBERT ORBAAN

Doubleday & Company, Inc.   Garden City, New York

ACKNOWLEDGMENTS

The author extends grateful thanks to the many persons and organizations who have given vital assistance in writing and illustrating this book.

To Richard Collier, E. P. Dutton & Co., Inc. and Wm. Collins Sons & Co. Ltd., for material re-told from their book, *Ten Thousand Eyes* by Richard Collier. Copyright © 1958 by Richard Collier.

To Jacques Lusseyran and Little, Brown and Company for material based on facts from their book *And There Was Light* by Jacques Lusseyran, English translation, Copyright © 1963 by Little, Brown and Company; Copyright © 1963 by Jacques Lusseyran.

To Doubleday & Company, Inc. and Curtis Brown Ltd. (New York), for material re-told from their book *An Army of Amateurs* by Philippe de Vomécourt. Copyright © 1961 by Philippe de Vomécourt.

To Doubleday & Company, Inc. for material based on *The White Brigade* by Bernard Goffin, translated by Charles Lam Markmann. Copyright 1944 by Robert Goffin.

To the staffs of various foreign information bureaus in New York City, notably Mr. Rolf Bergendahl of the Norwegian Information Bureau, Mr. J. van den Bogaert of the Netherlands Information Bureau, and experts in the information services of Denmark, France, Luxembourg, Belgium and Great Britain. Various government organs in these countries also were most helpful.

Valuable advice was provided by Mr. Kai Winkelhorn, who served with the rank of U. S. Army lieutenant colonel in the American Office of Strategic Services during World War II, his activities linked with the underground fight in Denmark.

The friendly encouragement and advice provided by the editorial staff of Doubleday & Company, Inc., notably Miss Ruth Shair and Mrs. Leslie Nassau, substantially aided me in completing the assignment.

To the heroes and heroines of
the anti-Nazi underground, living and dead.

CONTENTS

PROLOGUE

Thou sure and firm set earth,
hear not my steps, which way
they walk, for fear thy very
stones prate of my whereabouts.

Shakespeare (*Macbeth*)

The hunters were numerous, well armed, stone-hearted, and stalked their quarry round-the-clock.

They hunted human beings—any man, woman, boy, or girl who flouted the harsh edicts of the tyrant with the postage-stamp mustache and the nightmare brain.

When the stalkers pounced on a prey the routine was merciless. If mere questioning of a prisoner—almost invariably accompanied by painful beatings—proved unsatisfactory, there were other methods. No leather-aproned medieval torturer could improve on these.

The most relentless hunters were the agents of the dread *Geheime Staatspolizei*—Secret State Police—better known as *Gestapo* and members of the *Abwehr*, the German Army's intelligence division.

Citizens of conquered countries were the hunted. They dueled heroically against the enemy month after month, year after year, always against tremendous odds. Their casualties were staggering. They were an army of shadows, terrifying, elusive, now victorious, now vanquished, but always imperishable.

1

Fires in the Fortress

> Dictators ride to and fro upon
> tigers which they dare not
> dismount. And the tigers are
> getting hungry.
>
> *Sir Winston Churchill*

By 1939 all the bolts had been tightened in the most formidable war machine yet forged by man.

Its banner was bright red with a hooked cross outlined blackly against a white circle. The main color motif was significant—the hues of blood and of night.

In that fateful year the machine's supreme commander, Adolf Hitler, gave the dread signal to attack and the theory of total war became a reality. With smooth coordination the German juggernaut swept into action in *blitzkrieg* tempo—lightning war—snuffing out the lights in Europe and elsewhere in the world.

First the helmeted Hitlerian legions surged against Poland. That country went down in smoke and flame late in 1939. Then, after a period of minor armed action on the western front, known as the phony war, or *sitzkrieg,* they smashed northward and westward in the spring of 1940. In the south, Hitler's main European ally, Benito Mussolini of Italy, also set his military machine in motion.

In less than a year the ravening Third Reich, which was designed to last a thousand years, seized more *lebensraum*—living space—than Germany had ever had before. As soon as his conquests were more or less consolidated, Hitler built a gigantic fortifications line in northwestern France. It was named the Atlantic Wall. In due time he proclaimed boastfully that this defense, plus German control of other areas, had transformed Europe into a fortress—*Festung Europa.*

In this fortress were millions of persons of different nationalities—French, Hollanders, Belgians, Danes, and others.

Almost overnight, engulfed by an avalanche of steel, they

were in the grip of one of the most fearful tyrannies in history. The shock of events at first left them stunned and confused. But this semiparalysis did not last for long. They had known freedom and decency before the self-styled master race marched in. With each passing day their hatred for the Nazi conquerors blazed higher. Their determination to do something—anything—against the tyrants hardened everywhere.

Fires began to burn in the fortress. First in one country, then in another. Small fires at first, but flaring with increasing fierceness as months, years passed. Quenched in one spot, they broke out in another, and another, ignited and kept burning by armies of phantoms.

The citizens of conquered Europe kindled one of the most extraordinary struggles in history—the secret, or underground, war against Hitler in Nazi-occupied countries. Savage, silent, anonymous.

Although people have repeatedly battled oppressors by one means or another throughout history—the Boston Tea Party could be classified as a kind of underground operation—this large-scale duel in the shadows is unique. Its scope and duration exceeded anything previously recorded.

The threat of the underground, also widely referred to as the resistance, haunted the conquerors day and night. Sudden death from explosives, from a quick-firing hand weapon, from knife slash or swinging truncheon lurked everywhere for the "supermen."

The contribution of underground operations to eventual Allied victory over Hitler was great—railway communications thrown into chaos, telephone and telegraph wires cut, war production plants damaged, vital records destroyed and untold numbers of Germans killed in all types of attacks.

The underground heroes and heroines participated in adventures having all ingredients of fictional suspense stories. There were plots and counterplots, secret passages, false names and papers, undercover radio transmission, and breathtaking escapes from Nazi stalkers.

Resistance forces roughly fell into three categories.

Residents of a country involved were the vast majority.

Specially trained agents parachuted into a country or sent there in some other manner by the Allies composed the second group. This was mostly done by SOE—Special Operations Executive—created by the British with headquarters in London. Eventually the American OSS (Office of Strategic Services) headed by the late William "Wild Bill" Donovan, American World War I hero, joined in these operations. Governments-in-exile and the Free French of General Charles de Gaulle also were active in aiding the resistance in their particular country, in cooperation with SOE or OSS.

The third classification involved persons of foreign birth who were living in one of the countries and who, for one reason or another, decided to stay on or were unable to flee in time and became involved in underground activities.

The bulk of the underground battlers were young people—boys and girls in their teens or men and women under thirty. However, older persons, even the totally blind and other handicapped people, undertook hazardous assignments and did magnificent work.

Unlike combatants in most regular armed campaigns and battles they were in constant danger, continually on the run, harried ghosts, mostly wearing shabby clothes, often half-starved, striking with any means available.

The Nazis, notably the *Gestapo*, and the equally deadly *Abwehr*, held all the trump cards: fast cars, motorcycles, and airplanes; arms of all types; special car-borne detector apparatus which could almost immediately spot the location of an underground radio transmitter; control of the press, radio and telegraph, and full authority over the issuance of identity cards, food rationing books, or other papers required for daily living.

At any moment the Germans could dispatch swarms of soldiers or police agents to surround blocks of buildings or any other area for snap controls. Woe to any resistant caught in such a net.

At any place and time a German, sometimes in uniform, sometimes not, could accost a citizen of an occupied land with the nerve-wracking *Ausweis*—the order to show identification papers or other documents. Another German word became more feared than this one. It was *Aufmachen!* (open up), shouted by the hunters after banging on a door or doors in residential or other buildings, heralding a search or arrest. This German word was so pregnant with dire consequences that it created what was termed doorknob psychosis throughout occupied territory.

Constant patrolling made escape by land or sea very difficult and highly dangerous. Escapes by air were limited in number and effected in planes sent on special missions from Britain or other Allied territory. Border guards were numerous, aided at many points by savage dogs trained to kill or maim. Powerful searchlights could dispel the cloak of darkness. Another threat was ever-present—betrayal of escape attempts or other resistance activity by pro-Nazi citizens of an occupied land.

When captured there was no question of any mercy for resistants. The Germans simply labeled them terrorists. The firing squad, fiendish torture aimed at securing information, prisons and concentration camps such as Dachau, Buchenwald, or Ravensbruck faced captives suspected of anything but the most minor offenses.

The *Gestapo* stopped at nothing in its efforts to glean information which could help it stamp out opposition. Methods used in ancient times were resorted to and improved upon. Hour-long questioning accompanied by brutal beatings, immersions in ice-cold baths, floggings with whips having barbed-wire thongs, the use of thumbscrews, the bastinado (beating the soles of bare feet), steel head bands which could be tightened until the pain became unbearable, and electric shocks were some of the aspects of *Gestapo* procedure.

They invented an entirely new type of torture—the faked execution. All the moves of a formal execution were performed, except that the marksmen's rifles carried blanks or they suddenly lowered their arms after the victim clearly heard the commanding officer shout *"Feuer."* Then the dazed, shocked victim would be led back to prison. There are known cases in which this was done repeatedly, as many as nine times. Those who would not talk finally were really shot down.

Some prisoners were transformed into human icicles—thrown bound into specially constructed refrigerators until they were half-dead from freezing. This method was complemented by the use of hot rooms where the victim was subjected to escalating heat until it reached unbearable intensity.

All resistants were enjoined by their leaders to try to refrain from giving any information for at least forty-eight hours after arrest so that the enemy could not pounce too quickly on others in the particular group in which the captive was operating. An amazing number refused to speak at all, but those who survived and escaped death were sometimes crippled for life. Many did crack, half-insane from pain, and did reveal names, places, and plans. The Germans soon were in full cry, smashing one underground network after another. All action against the resistance was cunningly abetted by pro-Nazi traitors who infiltrated networks as spies or gave useful tips of various types to the Germans.

The real Nemesis of the resistance was not Der Fuehrer, who was born in Austria. This hunter was born German, Adolf's top police chief. His name was Heinrich Himmler—a strange little sadist with a somewhat commonplace appearance, totally at variance with any conceptions of Nordic supermen. His shadow was everywhere.

Himmler was head of the *Gestapo* and other police and the SS, or *Schutzstaffel*. The SS, originally a small elite guard for Hitler, eventually grew into a large body of men.

It became a kind of special army. Its members were the toughest, most rabid Nazis in existence.

Himmler also had wide authority in the operation of concentration camps where millions of Jews were liquidated in massacres unparalleled in history.

It was Himmler who conceived one of the most frightening edicts of all time, which was fully approved by Hitler. It bore resemblance to the *lettres de cachet* (secret letters) and other powers whereby tyrants of old could make their enemies disappear forever in terrible dungeons without trial or hope of reprieve. In ancient castles the dungeons in which such victims usually were placed were known as *oubliettes* (roughly meaning forgotten place). Often, as in the famous Castle of Chillon on Lake Geneva, Switzerland, the *oubliettes* were fearful underground cells, devoid of windows, with a small hatchway in the floor above through which a prisoner was lowered. Once inside, the prisoner was frequently forgotten until he died and his body was ordered removed from the cell.

The Nazi decree was applied to all Reich-held territory in December 1941. In western Europe this included most of France and Belgium, Holland, Luxembourg, Norway and Denmark. The decree was known as *Nacht und Nebel Erlass* (Night and Fog Decree).

Its purpose, as the ominous title indicates, was to seize persons endangering German security who were not to be immediately executed and take them into Germany where they vanished without trace. No information about a prisoner's fate would be furnished to members of his or her family. This applied also to place of burial. The number of prisoners who disappeared as "NNs" will never be known. According to all available information only a handful ever came back alive to their native lands. Unquestionably a large number of them were resistance fighters of both sexes.

One of the most arresting pictures of Himmler, who had a cold, calculating brain and had been a chicken farmer in

Bavaria before his rise to power, was penned by a high German officer, Major General Walter Dornberger:

"He looked to me like an intelligent elementary schoolteacher, certainly not a man of violence. I could not for the life of me see anything outstanding or extraordinary about this middle-sized, youthfully slender man in gray SS uniform.

Under a brow of average height two gray-blue eyes looked out at me, behind glittering pince-nez, with an air of peaceful interrogation. The trimmed mustache below the straight, well-shaped nose, traced a dark line on his unhealthy, pale features. The lips were colorless and very thin. Only the inconspicuous, receding chin surprised me. The skin of his neck was flaccid and wrinkled. With a broadening of his constant, set smile, faintly mocking and sometimes contemptuous about the corners of the mouth, two rows of excellent white teeth appeared between the thin lips. His slender, pale and almost girlishly soft hands, covered with blue veins, lay motionless on the table throughout our conversation."

There is an intriguing factor involving family history in the sinister Nazi tableau.

Hitler's father, Alois, was born illegitimately to an Austrian peasant woman named Maria Anna Schicklgruber, in 1837. Five years later Maria Anna was married to a man who presumably was the father of the boy. His name was Johann George Hiedler.

When Maria Anna died in 1847, Johann vanished for some thirty years from the Waldviertel district in Lower Austria

The map shows where some of the principal episodes in this book occurred:

1. Caen	5. Aalborg
2. Paris	6. Copenhagen
3. Grenoble	7. Odense
4. Clermont-Ferrand	8. Oslo

where the forebears of the future Nazi all-highest had lived for generations.

Johann Hiedler never formally legitimized Alois, and the boy grew into adulthood known as Alois Schicklgruber. His wandering father eventually returned to the Waldviertel district but had changed his family name from Hiedler to Hitler. Names such as Hiedler, Huetler, Huettler, and Hitler ran in the family.

Johann belatedly legitimized Alois and from then on he was known as Alois Hitler. Klara Poelzl, third wife of Alois, gave birth to Adolf in the Austrian town of Branau-am-Inn, across the border from Bavaria, on April 20, 1889.

There always will be speculation as to whether Adolf Hitler's destiny might not have been different if he had been born Adolf Schicklgruber. The word has a comical sound in virtually any language. Thunderous shouts of "Heil Schicklgruber!" would tend to provoke merriment rather than any kind of awe.

When he was a youth Adolf Hitler confided to a friend that nothing had ever given him so much pleasure as this change in name some thirteen years before his own birth. Adolf expressed the view that the name Schicklgruber "seemed so uncouth, so boorish, apart from being clumsy and unpractical." He added that Hiedler "was too soft" but Hitler on the contrary "sounded nice and was easy to remember."

This matter of names provided the people of occupied territories with excellent ammunition in the psychological warfare against the Nazis. Scribbling "Heil Schicklgruber!" on walls or pavements or shouting the name within their hearing was a sure-fire irritant to German nerves.

There was another factor which was frequently seized upon by the underground to ridicule the oppressor. This was the report—never quite verified—that Hitler, in his drifting, bum-like youth, had at various times been a house-painter. Actually, Hitler had made a stab at being an artist with deplorable results. Imitating the actions of a housepainter is easier and provides more comical twists than duplicating those of a person painting or sketching. The housepainting act, featuring a wide variety of facial and bodily contortions, was a favorite one with the younger element in occupied countries. It could be executed quickly, simply, and clearly when Germans or pro-Nazis were within eyeshot. A leering getaway with fingers parted in the V for Victory sign usually terminated the performance.

Although incidents in the shadow war often had humorous angles, they always involved risks. Just how far the Germans would go to stop any resistance is shown in some of the prison terms handed down in Holland in the early Nazi-occupation phase.

Using foul language in connection with Hitler. Four months.

Distributing an anti-German poem. Eight months.

Playing soccer with a German officer's cap. Ten months.

Thrashing two German brewery foremen. Fifteen months.

Wounding a German soldier with a beer bottle. Three years.

The resistance operations fell broadly into the following categories:

Armed action against the enemy. This included sabotage of factories, airfields, railways, shipping, munitions depots, and truck convoys, and attacks against German troops, civil officials, police, and pro-Nazi traitors.

Publication of illegal newspapers, pamphlets, and books and their distribution through various channels. This was a constantly devastating weapon against Nazi propaganda and its doctored war news.

Organizing the escape routes from Nazi-occupied territory. This activity, somewhat reminiscent of the Underground Railroad for fugitive slaves in the Civil War, was eventually of tremendous scope. It aided all types of persons—fleeing Jews, stranded Allied airmen, soldiers or special agents or resistance personnel whose situation had become too dangerous and had been ordered to leave.

Strikes and slow-down movements among workers which hampered Nazi war production in occupied areas.

Forging all kinds of documents, notably identity papers, and destruction of potentially dangerous Nazi records.

Pursuing and executing traitors, both men and women, convicted of betraying the underground. Once caught, such traitors were tried swiftly in secret, if there was time to try them at all, and if convicted, either shot or strangled.

Facilitating air drops of arms and other supplies by parachute. Aerial operations included the landing and departure of planes in isolated areas. These planes sometimes brought in secret agents or evacuated resistance personnel or agents already in the zone who were threatened with almost certain arrest.

Espionage of all types.

This is just a broad outline of the main activities. There were very many facets—varying from country to country.

The role of the men and women of God was outstanding. Clergymen of all faiths again and again scored Nazi actions in sermons and writing, often paying for their bravery with imprisonment and death. Catholic nuns and monks played heroic roles in aiding escapees to get out of an occupied country or providing hiding places for resistants. Often those befriended by the church were provided with clerical apparel and necessary false identity papers.

In ancient times churches and convents were sanctuaries for men or women who sought refuge from the law. During the Nazi occupation convents and monasteries helping fugitives used the very same secret chambers and passages which had permitted escapes centuries before. One convent in the Paris zone had an old dried-up well with a hiding place which had been built into the brickwork. Another convent made good use of a recess in the wall of its refectory. It was covered by a large painting of the Madonna and Child that could be opened like a door. A passage led from the recess to a tunnel which emerged at a spot well outside the convent walls.

While this book is concerned with the countries of western Europe, heroic exploits also took place in conquered Poland, occupied Russia, in the Balkans, and in Austria and Czechoslovakia. The latter two countries had been seized by Hitler prior to the outbreak of war. There also were various underground activities in Germany and Italy—including ill-starred plots to kill Hitler—but these do not come under the category of resistance to occupation by an invader. Both Hitler and Mussolini were legally in power in their own countries.

Resistance movements in the beginning were far from cohesive, interlocking organizations directed by centralized leading bodies. For most of the war's duration the underground consisted of scores of organizations under many names, most of the time operating independently of one another. Only in the latter months of the Nazi occupation were the various segments brought together, their activities coordinated by a central leadership council in whatever country they were operating.

One of the best descriptions of the embryonic development of resistance—truly applicable to any country—was penned by Jorgen Haestrup, noted Danish historian who was a member of Denmark's wartime underground.

"The origins of the Danish Resistance can neither be exactly localized nor precisely dated," he wrote in *Panorama of Denmark* published after the war by the Danish Foreign Ministry's Press Department. "Its earliest sources are untraceable and vanish into a fine network of innumerable, long-since dissipated moods, deliberations, resolutions and—eventually—action. A remark, a confidential talk, an arrangement—a demonstrative act. Later, or perhaps at the same time, a leaflet, a private meeting, a 'V' sign, an attempt to start a fire or steal weapons. . . .

"Always of trivial account singly, in the aggregate slowly perceptible. One day something tangible . . . resistance had to gather drop by drop, realizing itself as a movement through an imperceptible accumulation of innumerable isolated acts of private initiative, which lacking directives, often gropingly proceeded through resolution to action and slowly united in a common beginning."

The need for utmost secrecy and deception was constant. No effective provisions had been made for this kind of conflict in peacetime. There were no secret arms caches or hidden supplies. Contact between groups of resistants, if there was such contact, was very often entrusted to only two people. Frequently neither liaison agent knew the names or even met the other persons involved. Thus, under torture, not many names or other information could be given away.

All full-time resistants worked under aliases and carried false papers. Others did not go fully underground but kept their regular jobs and real names as long as this could be done, which, most of the time, was not too long. All kinds of disguises were used—false beards and mustaches, hair dyes, cotton stuffed into the mouths to alter cheek contours, even plastic surgery when such was deemed necessary.

A country's type of terrain also was of vital importance. Mountainous and heavily wooded areas were best for launching armed attacks or as hiding places. Norway had the best terrain in this respect, France second. Holland, Luxembourg, Belgium, and Denmark are relatively flat, although they have sizable forested zones. Generally, the best operational base aside from mountains was a large city where the resistant's intimate knowledge of various streets and houses made possible a quick getaway if necessary.

Favorite shooting weapons were revolvers, automatics, the easily assembled Sten gun and the American Army .30 caliber carbine when this became available in the latter half of the war. The best explosive was the plastic bomb which had the consistency of putty and could be detonated with a pencil-like time fuse. As far as transportation was concerned, bicycles were invaluable to the underground since Nazi regulations made it extremely difficult to use any automobiles or obtain gasoline. Skis also proved effective in mountain zones.

There was one swift, final escape when someone had been captured or knew that it was imminent and inescapable—suicide. This escape was a pill carried by many resistants. It was a cyanide pill. Swallowed, death was almost instantaneous. Many chose escape by suicide rather than be forced to talk. It was obligatory for all special agents sent out from Britain to carry this pill.

As in all human undertakings, money was needed, especially for full-time resistants who had forfeited all regular earning capacities and occasionally for bribing key German officials of the more avaricious type, of which there was no scarcity. The Allies were able to funnel in large sums via agents. In some cases people had sufficient savings and managed to live on them. Many full-timers were kept going by various small donations from friends. Some received large donations from wealthy persons also involved in secret operations but generally not suspected or particularly pestered by the Nazis.

Since France is the scene of the first detailed accounts in this book, a brief sketch of the situation there, roughly from 1940 to 1942, is desirable. At first the French people had been left punch drunk by the overwhelming conquest in 1940 and the sudden collapse of practically everything representing a normal way of life to them. Resistance of any kind seemed hopeless, even the whole Allied cause seemed doomed. The country was split at first into two zones. The northern area, including Paris, and a broad coastal belt down to Spain, was in the Nazi grip, known as the occupied zone. The southern part was under the doddering Marshal Henri Pétain, World War I hero of Verdun, and his collaborationist Vichy regime. This area, generally referred to as unoccupied France, would also be overrun by the Germans in the fall of 1942.

In France, as elsewhere, radio played a vital role for the first time in a major conflict by providing the conquered with news not issued by the enemy. The role of the British Broadcasting Company in this phase of the war was outstanding. Virtually everyone listened to the BBC news even though it was forbidden by the Germans.

Despite doctored Nazi accounts, the French soon realized that the Luftwaffe of German Air Chief, Hermann Wilhelm Goering, had taken a terrible trouncing from the British Royal Air Force and that there would be no Nazi invasion of that island bastion. This development proved a vital tonic for sagging morale throughout occupied lands.

The French also had an inspiring beacon of their own, also a hero of the battle of Verdun, General Charles de Gaulle. From de Gaulle, head of the Free French regime in London, came many fiery words, among them the famous statement: "France has lost a battle. But France has not lost a war." The stirring words of Winston Churchill and eventually those of President Franklin D. Roosevelt also fanned the flames of unrest in *Festung Europa*.

As resistance developed a word defining a certain type of terrain became widely used in France in regard to underground operations. It was *Maquis*—a Corsican term for high, thick brush that covers the hills of that country. In Corsica, when a man leaves home for one reason or another and goes into hiding, it is customary to state that he has taken to the maquis. Perhaps the best equivalent in our language is "take to the hills." In the course of the French occupation, resistants were referred to as persons in the Maquis or as Maquisards, especially those men who formed armed attack bands to strike at the Nazis.

By the spring of 1942 resistance, including many types of sabotage against communications and manufacturing plants, was daily gaining ground. Special agents had been landed in large numbers and were cooperating with various resistance formations in both zones.

One of the cruelest measures in the Nazi retaliatory arsenal was repeatedly carried out. This was rounding up groups of hostages and executing them in punishment for resistance attacks. Systematic pillaging of the occupied zone was in full swing. Near-starvation conditions prevailed for the French almost everywhere while all the Germans lived well. Deportation of tens of thousands of Frenchmen for slave labor went on unceasingly.

In spite of this tragic situation hopes of eventual liberation were higher than ever among most of the French. Some of the reasons for this were the United States' entry into the war, German difficulties on the Russian front, and Allied bombings. The German thrust against the Soviets had bolstered underground activity. The Communists, numerous in France, had been somewhat lukewarm toward any anti-Nazi operations as long as all was ostensibly rosy between Hitler and Russia's dictator, Joseph Stalin. The moment Hitler scrapped his friendship pact with Russia, the French Communists also became active in the underground. They proved to be brave Frenchmen in general, although many non-Communists wondered whether they took up the cudgels more for the purposes of Communism than patriotic reasons.

The first story of the resistance is set in France. It is a story of exceptional daring, a typical example of how resistants dueled with their wits against the Nazis. The whole operation has a vital link with the Allied invasion of 1944 which cracked *Festung Europa* wide open and paved the way for the Nazi and Fascist Armageddon.

2

France

To arms! to arms! ye brave!
The avenging sword unsheathe!
March on! March on! all hearts resolved
On victory or death!

*From "La Marseillaise," the French
national anthem, composed in 1792
by Claude Joseph Rouget de Lisle*

THE MEN WHO PLAYED
DOMINOES

Housepainter's gamble

Four eyes shadowed by the brims of steel helmets were closely observing Monsieur René Duchez on the sunny Thursday morning of May 7, 1942, in the town of Caen in Normandy, Nazi-occupied France.

The eyes belonged to two stony-faced German sentries posted in front of a building in the Rue Bagatelle, in the heart of the ancient city. Bayoneted Mauser rifles cradled in their arms, the two soldiers in field-gray uniforms were standing a few paces from Duchez, who was wholly engrossed in an activity of his own. The Frenchman, a native of the town, was performing the physical movements of a housepainter at work. At this moment—destined to prove important in the history of World War II—Duchez was plying a broad paint brush with frenetic vigor against a man-high wooden wall adorned with a swastika emblem.

There was something Chaplinesque in his performance. The actor, short and frail of build was wearing a frayed shirt and outsize, paint-daubed overalls which plopped over tattered sneakers. A silly grin played under his postage-stamp mustache.

Duchez was not doing anything very unusual. He was a

housepainter. But to the German eyes the scene did not look quite as it should. The brush had no paint on it. The wall he was painting—one of the wooden partitions of a black-and-white sentry box—visibly needed none. The whole box was bright and spotless. In addition, the Frenchman's activity smacked of sly anti-Nazi psychological warfare although Duchez was not aware of it at the time.

The Frenchman was actually applying for a decorating job which German authorities wanted done in the building the sentries were guarding. The two Germans, however, were in grave doubts as to just what he wanted due to linguistic difficulties. A crisis was imminent.

Early that morning Duchez had spotted a notice in French on the bulletin board outside the *Mairie*, the Caen city hall. The German authorities asked for decorators to submit estimates to the City Hall for minor painting and decorating work. This work was to be done at the Caen headquarters of the Nazi Todt organization which dealt with labor and construction work, the same organization which had built the mighty Siegfried defense line in Germany.

Although the notice had set a final date for submission of estimates at 5:00 P.M. the previous day, Duchez decided he would investigate anyhow. The housepainter entered the main hall of the *Mairie*, whistling disconnectedly as was his custom.

After some queries he was directed to a French official handling the matter. The official smiled when Duchez ambled up to his desk, a Gauloise cigarette dangling from his lips. He knew the little housepainter as most of the people in Caen did. Over the years Duchez—he was forty at this time—had become something of a local character, a hard-working man, jovial and witty, always welcome at a café gathering in hours of relaxation.

"I would like to have a try at that Todt proposition," Duchez said, his eyes twinkling. "You know I am not only good, but a great master when it comes to painting, paper-

hanging and the like. You know we need work in these
times."

"My dear Duchez, I am afraid you are a bit late," the official replied, shaking his head. "All the estimates were
turned in some twenty-four hours ago. However, there may
still be a chance. The Germans have not told us yet that
they have accepted any estimates. However, why don't
you go over there direct and see what you can do? It may
not be too late. Audacity, always audacity as our Marshal
Foch used to say, eh!"

Duchez agreed with this advice and with a friendly farewell left the building. Entering the small truck he used for
his work, Duchez headed for the Rue Bagatelle where the
Todt organization had its offices.

The Todt organization in Caen was not of prime importance in Normandy, being a subsector of the main headquarters at Saint-Malo. It had taken over three buildings in
Caen, one for camouflage, one for administering forward
personnel, and a third for operations involving map making
and works contracts. Without quite realizing it, Duchez
headed for the most important one as far as impending
events were concerned. It was the *Abteilung Technik*, the
offices handling maps, in a four-story stone mansion facing
directly on the Rue Bagatelle.

After a short drive, Duchez arrived at an opening in a
picket and barbed-wire fence extending some fifty yards beyond the building. He left the truck and smiled vapidly at a
nearby German sentry standing in front of his box. This
kind of smile was a speciality of Duchez in all dealings with
Germans. The soldier immediately strode toward him.

"Halt! *Ausweis!*" he barked, pointing his rifle menacingly
at the Frenchman.

Duchez fumblingly brought out his *Ausweis* from an over-
all pocket and began explaining that he wanted to apply for
a painting job according to the notice posted at City Hall.
The sentry did not know French nor could he understand
Duchez's hodge-podge German. He shook his head and mo-

tioned that Duchez should go away. Hearing the argument, which was noisy, another sentry came up to investigate. Duchez tried to explain the matter to him, but to no avail.

Anxious but undaunted, Duchez then pulled a paint brush from one of the pockets in his overalls, dodged past the two men, strode up to the sentry box and applied his brush to one of its sides. He complemented this action by pointing to the building with his free hand and declaring loudly *"Will arbeit* (Want work)."

At first the Frenchman's maneuver, which was executed with comical enthusiasm, was viewed with astonishment and a tinge of amusement by the Germans. But in less time than it takes to tell, this turned to anger, embodied in a string of choice German Army swear words. His face purple, one of the sentries stepped forward and sent Duchez staggering with a slap. Then both soldiers collared him and with some hard kicks to his backside, hustled him into the building. Once inside, they requested a monocled *Hauptbaufuehrer* (Todt captain) to investigate the matter, explaining their problem in rapid German, incomprehensible to Duchez.

The captain gave a long hard look at the rumpled Frenchman, whose cheek still flamed from the slap. Then, having some command of French, he asked him threateningly whether he was aware of what it meant to do pantomimes spoofing the Nazi all-highest.

Duchez, who actually had not intended to add to the long list of jokes about Hitler's past, then fully realized what had happened. Although bubbling with internal laughter, he managed to keep a straight face and gravely told the captain that no insult had been intended. He hastily added that he was a housepainter in search of work and was interested in submitting an estimate for the task listed at City Hall.

The captain smiled thinly, dismissed the sentries, and had Duchez interviewed by a Todt lieutenant who had a knowledge of French and knew about the work. The lieutenant told him that it was a simple papering assignment, involving two offices on the second floor.

Asked to submit an estimate, Duchez did some rapid thinking. Knowing pretty well what his competitors would be charging, he decided that he would have to undercut them badly. He did so reluctantly for reasons which would have caused his immediate arrest if known to the Germans.

"Twelve thousand francs,"* he answered, aware that this was surely one-third less than those of any competitors.

"That is reasonable," the officer said. "Now report to *Bauleiter* (Major) Schnedderer on the second floor."

The major, a powerfully built, bald-headed man with a dueling scar on his cheek, received Duchez cordially. The fact that Duchez' breath smelled of Calvados, a kind of local applejack, and that he appeared somewhat tipsy did not seem to disturb him. Duchez, however, was not drunk. His brain was working rapidly and clearly. He had downed a goodly quantity of the spirits, as usual, the night previous, but pretended alcoholic fogginess was part of the bag of tricks he used to make the Germans believe he was something of a fool.

Motioning Duchez to sit down in a chair, the major, who was wearing a gray uniform with a swastika armband, then talked at length about the patterns he would like for the offices involved, which were not his own. The Frenchman could never quite figure out why Schnedderer was so preoccupied with the decoration of offices occupied by others. He eventually concluded that the major was a frustrated interior decorator.

"Perhaps blue cannons against a yellow background, or blue horsemen against white," the major said. "Anything nice you can provide that has a military flavor."

Duchez nodded amiably, accepted a small cigar tendered by the unusually friendly German, and said he would do his best, promising to return the following day, Friday, May 8.

Duchez left the building with a perky whistle on his lips

---

* It is difficult to assess this sum in dollar value. The rate possibly was two to three dollars for every thousand Francs.

and a somewhat ambiguous parting grin for the two sentries. He then headed his battered truck for his workshop to seek some wallpaper samples which might prove satisfactory on the morrow.

The domino players

The Frenchman was elated. He had the job and something interesting might come of it. The Germans did not know of his secret rank, conferred on him in April when the first truly important French underground cell had been formed in Caen.

This grouping included seasoned resistance leaders and aides having effective contact with the underground in Paris and the Free French of General Charles de Gaulle in London. Duchez had been designated chief of one of its four main operational divisions, namely P-1, the P standing for persons. This placed him in command of all part-time resistance operators in the Caen area. Not far from Caen was the port of Cherbourg and various beaches which in about two years would be given special names such as Utah, Omaha, Gold, Juno and Sword.

A few weeks previous, Hitler had issued his famous directive No. 41. It ordered the construction of a massive fortifications line to be known as the Atlantic Wall along the northwestern French coast. Preliminary work had started by early May.

The newly formed Caen resistance cell, or *reseau* (network) as the French called such underground formations, had been assigned one paramount task by London and Paris —obtain every possible scrap of information about the wall for the Allied command.

Before going home for dinner with his wife, Odette, who also was working for the secret group, the housepainter strolled to the Café des Touristes, 17 Boulevard des Alliés. Here every evening he sipped Calvados and met some friends, frequently joining in their seemingly everlasting game of dominoes. The café was typically French, an estab-

lishment of the more modest type with mirrored walls, bare
floor, tarnished red leather benches, simple chairs with wire
backs, and a long zinc bar. Its owner Paul Berthelot and his
wife could be trusted. Their disdain for everything German
was of the purest Gallic intensity.

Undistinguished as it was, the café was of vital importance
to the network. It was a good meeting place with apparently
nothing secretive about it. And it also was a mailbox. Here,
unobtrusively sipping Calvados, wine, or beer, the underground fighters hatched plans or exchanged information.

Seemingly a group of harmless French civilians in somewhat seedy clothes, they were long-standing customers, their
favorite game, dominoes. This all was in keeping with a fun-
damental axiom of the resistance men, or *clandestins* as the
French also liked to call them: keep everything normal, throw
the Germans off the scent.

The only German who regularly frequented the café was
a rather elderly Wehrmacht captain whose real name was
never known to the Frenchmen. They called him "Albert."
His presence at first had caused them some anxiety but they
soon found out that he did not understand any French at all.
It was decided that his presence would be a shield. What
anti-Nazi would be daring enough to conspire under the
nose of a German officer? When the Frenchmen saw him
they usually gave him a *"bonjour"* or *"bon soir"* depending
on the time of day, their voices casual but courteous. "Albert," who always sat alone, would nod affably and continue
sipping his cognac.

In the basement of the café, a dirty, broken-down boiler
was one of the network's main mailboxes, a safe hiding place
for all kinds of documents containing vital information.
From here this information could be funneled to Paris and
conveyed to London either by illegal radio transmission or
secret couriers.

The immediate chief and organizer of the Caen group
was Marcel Girard, one of France's outstanding underground chieftains. Girard appeared in Caen at irregular in-

tervals, shuttling by train between Paris and Normandy under false papers stating he was a dealer in cement. In the
capital he was in constant touch with various other resistance
leaders, including Gilbert Renault.

Arriving at the café, Duchez ordered a generous Calvados
from Berthelot and then sauntered over to the domino players, not forgetting to give a *"bon soir"* to "Albert" who
was there as usual for his evening *apéritif*. There were half-
a-dozen players present, including Léon Dumis, an ex-garage
proprietor, Roger Déschambres, a plumber, and Eugene
Meslin, an engineer. The number of players was always kept
low to avoid suspicion, but certain ones always were present
in the evening in a cleverly organized rotation system.

While displaying intense interest in one of the domino
games, Duchez said quietly to Dumis:

"Eh! what do you know, I got some real *boulot* (French
slang for work) today. I am reporting there with some wallpaper tomorrow. It should do. It's this outfit."

He flipped a small piece of paper on the table; written on
it was the word Todt, which also means death in German.

"It should prove interesting," Duchez muttered.

The other men were promptly informed and made it clear
by various grunts and swift facial expressions that it was,
indeed, an interesting development. Thus far the network
had not been very successful in getting information about
Atlantic Wall plans. All knew that the Todt organization
was the main directing body in such work. This might prove
a break, with good luck.

"One thing, René. We know you. You're a reckless devil
and your favorite sport is baiting these Germans," Dumis
said. "Be careful. Really, sometimes you go too far."

"Ah, don't worry, Léon. I will, I will," Duchez replied
with a chuckle. "I can always fool them. They always think
I am a harmless, half-tipsy fool. I can handle them, don't
worry."

As darkness fell the café emptied and the sinister hush
caused by wartime black-out and curfew regulations fell on

the ancient town of cobbled streets, closely packed, red-tiled houses and soaring church spires. At dinner René informed his wife of the new development.

That night the fates—wherever they meet—were stacking some very lucky dominoes for Duchez and the desperate French underground war as a whole.

Touch and go

The next day, May 8, Duchez drove through the streets of Caen shortly after 9:00 A.M., pondering a final admonition from his wife, Odette, to be careful and vigilant.

Occasionally he would wave and shout a salutation to persons he knew as his truck bounced noisily through the streets which were by that time fairly crowded with local residents, farmers from nearby districts, and German soldiers. In his truck there was a rather bulky sample book of various types of wallpaper which he could supply and painting equipment. No sample was quite what Schnedderer wanted. There was one, however, with a greenish background showing a shako, crossed swords, and a drum which might do. To be true it was Napoleonic military equipment, but, so what? It was military and that should be good enough for that bald-headed, scar-faced German pig, Duchez reflected.

There were no complications for Duchez in entering the building of the Todt organization this time, and he was immediately taken to Schnedderer. After politely doffing his dirty beret, Duchez exchanged greetings with the major, and laid his pattern book on the officer's big desk.

The German immediately began scanning the various samples, obviously somewhat captivated by the Napoleonic one, which was near the top. He had hardly done so, however, when there was a sharp knock on the door and a young officer entered, bearing a rather large bundle of what seemed to be documents of some kind. With a snappy "Heil Hitler!" he laid the bundle on the major's desk and departed, heiling again.

Schnedderer, apparently forgetting briefly that Duchez

was standing near the desk, moved the wallpaper book aside and began to unfold the newly delivered bundle. The Frenchman, while pretending to admire the view, was watching Schnedderer out of the corner of his eye.

The major unfolded one of the documents on top of the pile and began studying a section of it. Duchez quivered but did not change his listless, disinterested facial expression. These were no routine documents. They were maps and the one being scanned by the officer seemed to be the biggest, with many folds!

With some quick glances the Frenchman, who could only see the back of the map section being scanned, perceived white lines against blue. There could be no mistake about what he saw. There was the mouth of the Seine and the outline of the coast at Honfleur, and near the noted seashore resorts of Trouville and Deauville, south of Le Havre and about fifty miles from Caen. His heart pounding, Duchez realized that he was looking at a Todt organization map of the coastline of Normandy!

The major's map scanning was a quick one. He folded the map again and pushed the whole pile to the left-hand corner of his desk, which was nearest to Duchez. Then he resumed his study of the pattern book.

Now came a series of developments which could have been part of a suspense play on the stage of a theater. While various thoughts raced through Duchez' brain, there was another knock on the main door of the room. A sergeant stepped in, saluted with another *heil*, and said something to the major which the Frenchman could not understand. Then the sergeant left, closing the door behind him.

Obviously acting on the information he had just received, the major almost immediately rose from his chair and headed for a second door just behind his desk, leading to an inner office.

The major opened the door and, leaning against the jamb, began dictating some kind of message to a clerk or secretary in the room beyond.

The major's back was now turned toward Duchez. He was alone with the maps, the major some six yards away. Whoever was in the other room could not perceive anything in the major's office.

This situation was too much for the Frenchman. Jittery but determined, he quietly slipped up to the desk and lifted a section of the map which had been studied by the officer. The major droned on. What Duchez saw convinced him that here was something of extraordinary importance.

The map was printed by the ozalide system of mimeograph, on deep blue cartographic paper, apparently a blueprint for some kind of defense construction. In one corner of the fold which the Frenchman was looking at was printed in big red letters SONDERZEICHNUNGEN—STRENG GEHEIM (SPECIAL BLUEPRINT—TOP SECRET). Elsewhere were such words as *Blockhauss* (blockhouse), *Stuetzpunkt* (strong point), and *Sofortprogram* (highest priority program).

Almost immediately he folded back the map and tensely watched the major. Even to be caught prying as he had done could have dire results. The housepainter made a fast decision. He picked up the bulky map and hurriedly looked around the room for an emergency hiding place. There was an open fireplace but that would not do, he decided. Above it, however, was a heavy mirror about two feet square, in a gilt frame, its base flush with the wall, its top part tilted slightly forward.

Fortunately, the room was carpeted and Duchez was wearing *espadrilles* (rope-soled sneakers). Map in hand, he stepped quickly to the mirror and slipped the map behind it. Unless someone went and peered behind the mirror the map could not be easily spotted. Silently Duchez walked away and looked indolently out of one of the windows at the streets of Caen and passersby immediately below.

He felt weak in the pit of his stomach. Any unfavorable coincidence now would prove a delight to the effeminate, sadistic Helmut Bernard, head of the Caen *Gestapo*. He claimed he could make anyone talk and had proved this in the past. Various inexperienced resistance groups functioning in Normandy had been crushed one after another with torture and executions. Duchez could expect the very worst for what he had just done.

Fortunately for Duchez the maps were of somewhat the same formation and bulk. A hasty glance at the pile showed him that removal of the top one had not noticeably altered the bundle.

Completing his dictation, the major closed the door with a bang. Returning to the desk, he again leafed through the pattern book and selected the Napoleonic wallpaper and another.

"Come back on Monday and start work," Schnedderer said to Duchez, who had resumed a respectful attitude in front of the desk.

Duchez nodded politely and prayed silently that he would get out of the building with a whole skin. The officer then calmly began reading some other papers on his desk, apparently not suspecting anything.

The housepainter left the room and walked down two flights to the street in something of a trance, largely one of fear. He expected any minute to hear the pounding of hobnailed boots and feel the thud of a gun butt in his back or face. Nothing happened, however.

The entire affair had lasted less than an hour. Duchez hurried to the Café des Touristes and downed a stiff dose of Calvados to calm his frayed nervous system. None of his resistance comrades were there and Duchez did not mention what had happened to Paul, the owner.

That afternoon he told Odette about his coup. Duchez had done various minor anti-Nazi deeds during the past and Odette took it calmly.

"And now, what next, my dear husband?" she asked. "You know the old saying 'so long does the pitcher go to the well.' It's fine to have the map where it is but how to get it away from there?"

"Oh, I will find a way, don't worry. I've got a cool head," Duchez replied airily.

That evening before curfew at 7:30 P.M., Duchez arrived at the Café des Touristes where the usual game of dominoes was in progress, some six men present. He informed them of what he had done. "Albert" was sipping his drink in his usual chair, paying scant attention to the chatter of the Frenchmen.

Fernand Arsene, the one-eyed plumber who was one of the sturdiest resistants in the area, held that the entire episode was a figment of Duchez' imagination, just a joke. Others believed him. All, however, agreed to keep silent about it and await developments.

That weekend passed quietly at the Duchez home, René playing with his children, Jacques, eleven, and Monique, three, and discussing various events with his wife. He briefly visited the café but the Todt affair was not discussed.

There was no shout of *"aufmachen"* at the door. No alarm of any kind.

Something serious had happened in Paris, however, although the men of Caen were blissfully unaware of it at this time. The *Gestapo* had struck hard, the blow leveled at the *Confrérie de Notre Dame* (Brotherhood of Our Lady), the network headed by Renault. It was this network working in cooperation with the OCM (Civil and Military organization) that was directing the operations in which Duchez and his friends were involved. Marcel Girard who was the chief link between Paris and Normandy and organizer of the Caen group, also belonged to the OCM.

The chief radio operator of Renault's network had been captured. He had struck a bargain with the *Gestapo* to avoid torture and had named names. Several key men of the *Confrérie* had been seized but fortunately had not cracked thus far. Nonetheless, Girard and Renault and all others in the two networks were in graver danger than ever before.

Thousands of *Gestapo* agents in Paris were hot on the

scent. There was no certainty that the events in the capital might not lead to revelations pointing to Caen and the Atlantic Wall.

The Duchez touch

At about 8:00 A.M. on Monday, May 11, René entered the Todt building with buckets of sizing, the selected rolls of wallpaper, and other equipment of his trade. He started work immediately in one of the two rooms which had been designated, washing the walls down to the plaster and sizing them.

Sometime during the morning he contacted an orderly who could speak some French and told him that he would like to see Major Schnedderer for a few minutes. Somewhat to Duchez' consternation, the orderly told him that Schnedderer had been transferred permanently to Saint-Malo. What did this mean? Had something been discovered? René reflected anxiously.

"He has been replaced by Major Adalbert Keller and he is far too busy to see you now. Go ahead with your work," the orderly said grumpily and stalked away.

While working away at the task on hand, Duchez torturously weighed one idea after another throughout that Monday. Plainly, if something were to be done he would have to do it, somehow. Any attempt to enter the building in some secret fashion and pilfer the map was out of the question. There always were watchful eyes present. Although he was in the building, the little Frenchman could not swiftly sneak into the room with the mirror. Keller or somebody was always in it. The housepainter at this moment had no truly valid reason for seeing the high officer at all. Perhaps, the map already had been found and the Germans were checking up, with the finger of suspicion inevitably pointing at him.

Having completed one room, Duchez left the building about 4:00 P.M., leaving his buckets and paper on the premises. He was non-committal in a brief call at the café and

also when he returned home. Sometime before dawn a plan
hatched in his cunning brain.

He was in a markedly cheerful mood when he started
work on Tuesday in the second room. About 10:00 A.M. he
deferentially contacted the young lieutenant in charge of the
papering job. Would the lieutenant kindly inform him when
Major Keller would allow him to start work in his office?

"What work?" the lieutenant replied sharply. "Never
heard of anything to be done in that room."

But, yes, Duchez lied, it had all been arranged when he
conferred with Schnedderer the previous week, a bit of extra decorating.

The upshot was that within half an hour or so Duchez,
the lieutenant and a clerk were in the room with the mirror.
Keller was not there at that moment. The Germans insisted
that there was no order for this extra job. Duchez with
equal persistence maintained that Schnedderer had instructed
him to paper his office, had even selected the wallpaper.

Irritated by the stubbornness of the Frenchman with the
dumb facial expression, the two Germans began to do some
desk-thumping accompanied by loud expostulations.

Duchez noted with quick glances that the mirror area
apparently had not been searched. Suddenly the door behind the desk opened and Keller strode in, a tall, youngish
man with blond hair and ice-cold blue eyes.

"What is all this about wallpaper?" he asked in German.
Then in French, addressing Duchez: "And you, what's your
name and what do you want?"

Stating his name in an obsequiously polite voice, Duchez
assumed an extremely puzzled and injured look and repeated
his story. Keller pondered a few seconds and then stated
that he knew nothing of such work and doubted whether
the budget called for it.

"Ah, there is no question of money, Major Keller,"
Duchez exclaimed. "I have not made it clear. I offered to
paper this room free of charge, a gesture of goodwill toward
Major Schnedderer and all the personnel of Todt. After all,

he did assign me to the other job, which came in handy."

The major's heart was touched. There was precious little goodwill for the Reich in France and elsewhere in Europe. The officer smiled and gave Duchez a friendly pat on the shoulder.

"Fine, you can start tomorrow when I will be out of the office most of the day," he said.

Duchez told him he thought he could do the job in a day. The major informed him he would have all the furniture removed from the room that evening.

If the map was still behind the mirror this would have serious results. Duchez kept cool and thought fast again. Would the major have desk, chairs, and rugs placed in the center of the room? Then he, Duchez, would cover them with his own dust sheets. As far as the mirror was concerned, he would take it down and replace it after that particular area had been papered. The major did not quibble about these points and nodded approval.

That afternoon Duchez completed his work in the other rooms. He left the building whistling loudly at about 5:00 P.M. He was convinced by now that the theft of the map had not been discovered, that it was still where he had placed it.

At the café that evening he was somewhat more voluble.

"Things are going pretty good. Tomorrow will tell the tale," he declared and said the same thing to his wife that night.

The following morning, Wednesday, May 13, he arrived early at the Todt building and proceeded directly to Keller's office. His request had been fulfilled regarding the furniture. A quick glance behind the mirror. The map was still there. Duchez worked at high speed till almost 5:00 P.M.

The work completed, he left the room with his equipment, reported to an orderly, and was told he could come back the next day for his payment of 12,000 francs.

Then Duchez left the building. With him went the map. After a brief stopover at his workshop, he headed for the

café, wearing a shabby topcoat. He was whistling again as
he passed *Gestapo* headquarters in the Rue des Jacobins with
its big red Swastika banner.

Sleight of hand

The usual game of dominoes was going on at the Café des
Touristes at about 5:30 P.M. of that memorable date in the
fight against the Atlantic Wall.

Three men of the resistance group, not counting the
café's owner, were present: Roger Déschambres, Léon Dumis, and Pierre Harivel, insurance agent. "Albert" also had
arrived and had sat down a few tables away after hanging
up his heavy military overcoat on a coat stand.

At that moment Girard also was walking toward the café,
having arrived by train from Saint-Malo. He had not given
any advance notice of this and knew nothing about "Operation Duchez."

The three players were conjecturing on what had happened in the Todt building when Duchez entered the café.
He gave them a casual greeting, hung up his topcoat next
to that of "Albert" and ordered a Calvados from Paul at the
zinc bar. Drink in hand he strolled over to the players and
sat down, saying nothing of importance.

Suddenly he pushed back his chair and sauntered toward
the door of the café, a Gauloise between his lips, his drink
in his hand. The three others looked at each other. What
was Duchez up to? Their assumed indifference now masked
mounting tension.

In the doorway, Duchez was watching something menac-
ing out of the corners of his eyes, although seemingly non-
chalantly interested in the activity of the nearby flower mar-
ket beneath St. Peter's church. A black Citroën with police
markings was heading slowly in the direction of the café. In
the back two men sat silently, wearing raincoats and felt
hats. The car was not visible to the domino players.

After observing the car for a few seconds, René turned
and re-entered the café humming loudly and discordantly.

ment," Duchez replied grinning. "When the *Gestapo* was around I went to my overcoat over on the rack, pulled a pack of cigarettes from a pocket and simultaneously transferred the envelope to Albert's overcoat. When he left I helped him on with his coat and got the envelope back. The *Gestapo* would not have searched him. Very safe, you see. A little sleight of hand is good at times."

Girard and the others could not help smiling at this. Shortly after six the other Germans left and so did Girard, heading for the railway station. In a capacious pocket inside his overcoat was the envelope and a batch of informative reports from various agents taken from the boiler mailbox.

The tin box

The trip to Paris was uneventful but far from restful. The train was crowded with various types of French passengers and German soldiers and inspectors. All aboard were plagued by uneasiness, not unusual in those times. The train might be wrecked at any time by resistance saboteurs. The Communist resistants were particularly active in this type of attack and frequently were not deterred by the fact that many French people might be on a train.

Some four weeks previous a German troop train on the Cherbourg-Paris line had been derailed. More than a score of Wehrmacht men were killed. Nazi reprisals were swift and terrible. Five hundred Communists, their names furnished by the police of the Vichy government, and five hundred Jews were picked up. They were never seen again. Execution squads accounted for some twenty other persons. No train now moved without a certain number of French people aboard. They were hostages.

During the trip Girard was asked twice to show his papers, but they were in order. He did not touch the map or other documents. "My God, if I had only known what a bomb was in that envelope," he told friends much later when the full importance of the map became known.

Arriving in Paris shortly before ten o'clock that night he

got past the inspectors without trouble. Then he hailed a
bicycle taxi and was borne in its side-car to his apartment
building on the Left Bank, in the Rue du Cardinal Lemoine.

Barely beating the ten o'clock curfew in Paris, he limped
slowly up six flights of stairs. One of his legs had been almost severed at the knee by Nazi bullets in the withdrawal
at Dunkirk and had never truly healed, even after operations
and months of hospitalization in 1940. Girard had three
apartments on this floor, all small ones. One was his official
residence but he never entered it. He always used one of the
other two, which were linked by an inner door. In the hallway was a skylight which could be reached by a small ladder—an escape route to his and adjoining roofs.

Having entered one of the two other rooms, whose windows carried blackout curtains, he lit a light and for the first
time studied the map. It was a map of the Normandy coast
all right, from the mouth of the Seine to just below Cherbourg. It was studded with all kinds of German words and
Girard's knowledge of that language was very slim. He did
understand such words as *Flammenwerfer* (flame thrower)
and *stuetzpunk* but could not grasp the entire meaning of
the map.

The next day he contacted other resistance leaders who
took it to the chief of the Operation Civile et Militaire. This
man, who knew German well, gasped when the map, about
ten feet long and two feet wide, was unfolded on a table
in his apartment.

This was a top-secret blueprint of the Atlantic Wall on a
scale of just over one inch to the mile! Coastal defense
points were charted in minute detail.

"I believe this may be the most important thing we have
obtained thus far," he told Girard and two other men present. "We must pass it onto Renault and his CND as soon as
possible."

One thing somewhat dismayed Girard and the others—
the fact that work on the Atlantic Wall had progressed
seemingly much farther than was generally known. They

could not realize that this was just a blueprint, that only some land clearing operations and some digging had been carried out to date.

That afternoon Marcel Berthelot, alias Lavoisier, ex-diplomat of France, handed the map in its envelope to Renault while both sat on the terrace of a Paris café. In a low voice he told Renault what the envelope contained. He also informed him that a comprehensive copy of it had been made by resistance draftsmen, but on a reduced scale. This was a precaution often taken to safeguard against loss or seizure of important original documents.

Now it was up to Renault, a short, stocky, bald man, to get the map out of France. This mild-mannered man, whose normal occupation involved the financing of motion pictures, was one of the most extraordinary men in any resistance movement. He had all the characteristics of a top-notch commander—cool nerves, keen intelligence, and selfless devotion for his men, every inch a patriot.

For Renault the picture was a somber one in May and getting worse hourly. The hounds were in full cry in Paris and would strike soon in Caen itself. Most of his radio operators had been seized. The *Gestapo* and the *Abwehr* were gaining more and more revealing information. One of the CND operators had swallowed a cyanide pill as he was arrested in one of the big boulevards. Others had been seized, some of them never to be seen alive again.

The *Gestapo* had good knowledge of Renault's physical appearance. Fortunately, they had not yet tracked down his wife and four children. They were residing in a small town in Brittany with friends. Although his wife and her friends were not directly involved in resistance work there was no reason here for any abatement of doorknob psychosis.

For many days it seemed as if the fates, which had smiled on Caen, were now frowning on anything having to do with the map. In mid-May, Renault and Robert Delattre, a radio operator, went to Brittany by train to arrange for sea transportation of the map and other documents to England.

In their baggage was the map, a heavy sheaf of reports from various agents, and a radio transmitting set. If a German detected any of this material it would brand them immediately as dangerous resistants.

Renault had a navy—if by the wildest stretch of the imagination it could be called that. It consisted of several stouthearted Breton fishermen and a boat—*Deux Anges* (*Two Angels*). The men were in excellent shape but the boat was not. She was a dilapidated fishing craft with two masts for sails or netting, her length about 35 feet. She had a 25-horsepower motor which had seen better days, its disposition anything but angelic. With both sails and motor working *Deux Anges* could achieve a top speed of 13 knots in very favorable weather.

First, Renault and his companion went to Lorient, Breton port city, to contact other resistance leaders and the crew of *Deux Anges*. Here they set up their transmitter in an attic apartment and tried to contact "Colonel Passy" (Captain Andre Dewavrin), chief of de Gaulle's Military Intelligence Division in London.

Delattre had barely started to transmit when Renault spotted a radio detector automobile prowling along a nearby street. Its disguise as an ambulance did not fool him. Transmitting was stopped immediately and he and Delattre scrambled downstairs with the set wrapped up in a bag. It was Renault's last remaining transmitting set. All others in Paris used by his network had been seized by the Germans or could not be put into operation because of increasingly heavy detector operations. The two men passed the dreaded car without incident and then headed for the nearby town of Baud and the house where Renault's family resided.

On Monday, May 18, Delattre contacted "Colonel Passy" and arrangements were made for a sea operation.

As in all resistance ventures, the odds in such an exploit were tremendous, the problems complex, every second loaded with danger. There was no question of *Deux Anges* going all the way to England. Gasoline had to be obtained from the Germans in carefully controlled quantities. The Nazis permitted fishing boats to go out to sea during daylight hours within a more or less prescribed zone. They had to pass control points, however, and there were watchful German fliers in the skies above and many fast patrol boats on the water. The *Deux Anges* would have to be contacted by a trawler sent from England. The movements of the trawler also had to be timed so that it would appear temporarily to be just another boat in the German-controlled fleet. Unlike underground action on land, weather here also was of tremendous importance. The danger was much greater on a bright, sunny day than on a foggy one.

A rendezvous at sea was arranged for Wednesday, May 20, at 4:00 P.M. Greenwich meridian time. Two other rendezvous were set for 10:00 A.M. and 4:00 P.M. on Thursday, May 21, in case something went wrong with the first one.

It had been decided that Paul Mauger, the youngest man in Renault's work, would go aboard the *Deux Anges* with the map and other documents chosen by Renault for transportation to England. The precious map had been placed by Renault in a very commonplace type of Breton biscuit tin.

The *Deux Anges* put out from Lorient to keep the first rendezvous with Mauger, his documents, and the map aboard. The frail craft had hardly gotten underway when the engine conked out. That scotched the first rendezvous because the motor could not be repaired before nightfall. There were the two rendezvous scheduled for the next day and the Frenchmen hoped they could succeed in one of them. But the fates blasted this. That night British bombers dropped mines at the entrance to Lorient port. The Germans promptly forbade all shipping to leave port until the channel had been swept.

Realizing this might take days, Renault decided to return to Paris with Delattre and Mauger and do something later. His continued presence in Baud was also a grave danger to his family. The tin box, all documents, and the transmitter were again on the train for the return trip.

More staggering blows awaited Renault in Paris. Delattre and Mauger were seized late in May and dragged to *Gestapo* headquarters, Delattre with a wound in his arm. Renault's gloom was deeper than ever, two of his finest men gone. They probably would not talk but one could never be sure. The grief-stricken CND leader had to adopt the attitude which was part of the psychological armament of all underground fighters. Consider those arrested as dead, finished. Do not think about them. Do not visualize the multiple horrors of the torture rooms—the screams, the sobbing and the ruthless *anschnautzen* (snorting), the favorite German word for describing various forms of questioning.

In June Renault's situation became untenable. The *Gestapo* found out that his family was in Brittany living near the coast. Comrades in Paris warned him that the *Gestapo* even knew that he wore matching ties and handkerchiefs. Two sisters of his residing in Paris were traced and questioned but not arrested. Dewavrin sent him a message ordering him to proceed to England with his wife and children and entrust CND to someone else, stressing that arrest was inevitable if he tarried much longer in France.

At the end of the second week in June, Renault again departed by train for Brittany with the tin box and various documents, accompanied by another radio operator. The journey was at night and Renault and his baggage were placed in a two-bunk sleeping compartment whose other tenant was a German officer. The German, however, proved not the least interested in the little Frenchman in the shabby clothes and faded beret.

The journey passed without untoward incident. The next day Renault was reunited with his family and told his wife that preparations were underway for all of the family to go to England aboard the *Deux Anges*. Contact was effected with London and rendezvous were decided upon for Wednesday, June 17, or Thursday, June 18.

It was decided that they would embark on the *Deux Anges* early Wednesday morning at Pont-Aven, a small fishing port on a river bank inland from Lorient.

The journey got underway as scheduled on Wednesday, a blend of chilling suspense and comical situations. The passengers numbered seven—the Renault family and a young resistant determined to join the Free French fighting forces of de Gaulle. The crew consisted of a stouthearted Breton seaman and Renault's chief liaison man in Lorient. Passengers were squeezed into narrow lockers or a diminutive hold about five feet square and two feet high. The tin box and other baggage also were placed in a locker. Everything stank of fish, particularly the hold. The passengers had about as much space to move in as someone in a coffin.

The morning mist was slowly evaporating, revealing patches of bright sky when the *Deux Anges* chugged away, only two men visible on her decks. The first big danger was only three miles away—a pier where all fishing boats had to halt for German inspection. The Germans made a thorough search of every second boat, in the other cases merely asking for a list of crew members. The fate of the *Deux Anges* here would depend on pure luck and all knew it except Michel Renault. Michel, who was eighteen months old, was snuggled up against his father in the hold.

This was one peril but Renault particularly was aware of another one. Michel was sleeping peacefully as the *Deux Anges* glided slowly alongside the pier. Renault and his wife Edith had planned for a contingency involving Michel. The father had a bottle of milk in his pocket. Michel awoke and Renault fumbled in his raincoat pocket and tried to get the rubber nipple into the youngster's mouth. In doing this some milk spilled on the baby's face and he laughed joyously. Renault tried again but the baby pushed the bottle away. It was not his regular feeding time and he simply did not want any of it. Michel then made other vocal sounds of considerable loudness. The skipper above heard the sound and deliberately raised the anchor chain, dropping it heavily on the wooden foredeck.

Ransacking his brain for some method of keeping Michel quiet, Renault remembered he had some chocolate drops in his pocket and succeeded in having Michel suck on one. This kept him quiet. By amazing good luck the *Deux Anges* was the last in line and it was the craft just ahead that was thoroughly searched.

The fishing boats then scattered in various directions and the *Deux Anges* headed for the rendezvous, latitude 47.37, longitude 4.2.

It was a clear day and as a result the passengers had to remain hidden. At one point a German patrol plane roared above the craft at a height of less than a hundred feet. At 4:00 P.M. the trawler was sighted and the *Deux Anges* drew alongside. There were no other fishing boats in sight. Their hearts filled with joy, the passengers were transferred to the trawler and the crewmen of the *Deux Anges* headed back toward France.

By Friday the armed trawler had reached the Scilly Islands. From there the seven were taken to London by Royal Navy motor torpedo boat and train. By Monday, June 22, the map and other stacks of reports were in the hands of Allied intelligence in London.

The housepainter's gamble had paid off.

There is some mystery to this day as to just when the Todt organization discovered the loss of the map. Blueprints for Normandy coastline defenses came to Caen via Todt headquarters in Paris and the Todt offices in Saint-Malo, after approval by Berlin. Batches of such maps, sometimes duplicates, sometimes not identical, were channeled to various offices besides Saint-Malo and Caen. Fortunately for "Century"—the name given to the Normandy resistance operation—the map pilfered by Duchez was in a batch of duplicates.

According to the British writer, Richard Collier, in his authoritative book on the whole Century operation, entitled *Ten Thousand Eyes*, Keller did in due time find out that one of the maps was missing. But he at first assumed that another department had retained it for study. His view was apparently shared by his superior in Caen, Major of Engineers Ott. Fully realizing that knowledge of such a loss might straddle them with charges of extreme negligence, both most likely decided to keep the matter as hush-hush as possible. The Caen *Gestapo* was not informed of the incident. Instead Ott and Keller sent their own Todt Security Squad into action in Caen in a series of hit-and-run raids, whose real intent was kept veiled.

The Todt Security Squad gave a terrific going-over to the Café des Touristes in June, weeks after Duchez' coup. However, they apparently had no inkling of just how close to the bull's-eye they were. They turned over chairs and tables, poked long spikes down into the stuffing of benches, searched behind the bar and questioned Paul the owner, who was on tenterhooks because of the boiler in the basement. The Germans never did scan the boiler, fortunately. Other cafés were searched, not only the premises but customers as well.

The owners of lodging-houses and hotels were closely questioned as to what guests they had had during that month and in May. By some fantastic streak of luck they never went after Duchez, although he had definitely been seen by numbers of persons in the Todt building and had collected his pay. Apparently his studied air of semi-idiocy and tipsiness had lulled suspicion. According to all reports, the somewhat amiable Schnedderer was never contacted and hence had no occasion to recall his talks with the little house-painter. Nothing came of the entire search.

The children get bored on Sunday

During ensuing months the Century operation was expanded until it included some five thousand operatives of various categories, part-time and full-time, both men and women. Piecemeal information on the development of the Atlantic

Wall defenses were gathered from everywhere and embodied in dispatches or translated into Century's own maps drawn up by skillful draftsmen. This information was funneled to England in due time by various means.

In October 1942, Renault returned to France to contact Girard in Paris. Girard could hardly recognize him. An expert make-up man of Denham Film Studios in England had remolded him in a manner which would have delighted Sherlock Holmes. Renault appeared to be a stooping, wrinkle-faced, elderly man, with a frazzled red mustache, a hunchback with a pot belly. The latter two disfigurements were caused by props under his clothing. By December, however, it was decided by London that in spite of the disguise it was too dangerous for him to stay on and he was ordered back, making the trip again in the *Deux Anges*. He was never permitted to return, much to his disgust.

In February 1943, "Colonel Passy" (Dewavrin), was parachuted into France to organize a National Council of the Resistance, which would effect cohesion between the five biggest groupings, OCM, Ceux de la Résistance, (Those of the Resistance), Ceux de la Libération, (Those of the Liberation), Libération, and Front National, the latter the Communist Party faction. In March 1943, this bore fruit and the National Council came into being.

Terror and tragedy were impending for the valorous French, who numbered tens of thousands in these various groupings. The *Gestapo*, the *Abwehr*, and SS men went into action in a massive offensive to smash all resistance throughout France. Arrests and torturings multiplied daily. So did the information in *Gestapo* files.

"Operation Grand Duke," as it was called, shook the resistance to its foundation. Dewavrin had returned to London but Girard and countless other leaders were in greater danger than ever before, hunted with such intensity that their effectiveness was considerably curtailed, for the time being at least.

The drive reached out into Normandy. In the fall of 1943 the *Gestapo* pounced on the house of Duchez. It is not quite clear to this day why the house was raided.

Duchez had been doing various types of dangerous work during previous months but had not come under suspicion. He had been particularly active in helping downed Allied aviators escape. In one instance this involved five Americans. Possibly René drew suspicion on himself by somewhat carelessly phoning a resistance comrade that the fliers had been safely shepherded to a designated area with the statement "have delivered five pots of paint." It is possible that Duchez, always reckless, may have given his name over the phone.

At the time the *Gestapo* struck Duchez was in his house with another resistance man talking with Odette. His quick intelligence saved him when the *Gestapo* men stomped in—but at a tremendous price.

He spotted the fact that the raiders apparently were new men in the area and did not know him by sight. He convinced them that he was another man seeking Duchez to discuss business. They let him go but he went with a breaking heart. He knew Odette would face terrible days because there were all types of incriminating documents in the house. His was one of those soul-searing decisions the people of the underground had to make. It was imperative that he escape. He knew many more names than did Odette. He immediately left Caen and obtained false identification papers and a new name.

Helmut Bernard, Caen *Gestapo* chief, personally took care of Odette. She was punched, kicked, and flogged with a horsewhip into unconsciousness time and again. But she never talked. Eventually she was sent to Mauthausen concentration camp, "the camp of no return." She survived, however, and returned to Caen and René after the war.

"Operation Grand Duke" was a hard blow but could not kill the French resistance. It grew in power every day, with its own secret armed bands famous today as the *Maquis*.

Sabotage of railways and communications and the bombings of industrial plants continued at an accelerated tempo.

The conviction that things were going badly for Hitler and that an Allied invasion of the *Festung Europa* was impending fanned the flames of revolt. More and more side-arms and explosives were dropped from the air, American planes donating heavy quotas.

In June 1944, the fateful message "the children get bored on Sunday" crackled across the air waves from London. It was the signal for all-out resistance attacks in support of the gigantic invasion of the Normandy coast.

The *clandestins* responded magnificently. Attacks against supply and troop trains intended to bolster the German lines in Normandy were hit at point after point.

What happened to *Apfelkern* would have made Hitler chew up a whole rug but it is probable that he never even heard about it amid the general chaos. *Apfelkern* (apple-seed) was one of the biggest train convoys ever assembled by Hitler's commanders in France. It consisted of some twelve trains loaded with thousands of troops and tons of supplies, including artillery and machine guns. French *cheminots* (railway workers) operated the railways under German supervision. They were determined that *Apfelkern* would never get to any useful point.

Its progress was blocked every time it got underway. Advised that it was going to move in a certain direction, the *cheminots* raided a small station named Saint-André which was on its route. The stationmaster was bound and gagged and slightly beaten up and scratched so that he could claim he had been attacked by the resistance. Then freight cars in the station were sent down an incline and derailed, blocking the line. The railwaymen, who had raided at night, were back at their jobs early the next morning. The Germans were advised there had been an accident along the line and that a crane would have to be provided. The Germans sent a crane but when it arrived at the scene it broke down,

skillfully sabotaged. The railwaymen then clamored for a larger crane, which was provided, and cleared the wreckage. This action already had caused almost a two-day delay. Now one section of the convoy, a locomotive, some 13 cars and the crane proceeded on its way. But not far. At nightfall it was attacked by the *Maquis* and *cheminots*. The crane was uncoupled and wrecked before the attackers withdrew. This was followed by further sabotage. Days of delay grew into weeks, so *Apfelkern* never did reach the battle front. The *cheminots* and their friends had scored one of the great sabotage feats of the war.

When the invasion of Normandy got underway Duchez, Meslin, Déschambres, Dumis, and other men and women who were helping them were in full action aiding the Allies, including the Americans. They had arms by now and knew how to use them, most of them having seen army service prior to the war. Girard was fleeing from the Paris area in the general direction of Normandy, accompanied by his comely and courageous secretary, Denise Geninatti-Banck, who gave him notable aid in his dangerous work. The two, traveling on bicycles, eventually reached safety in the lines of General George Patton's American tank forces.

Caen itself was devastatingly bombed, one of the buildings badly hit being the Café des Touristes where the men played dominoes.

As elsewhere in France, the men and women of the resistance received thousands of decorations for valor, both French and foreign after the liberation.

Duchez was honored by the Poles; by the Americans who bestowed on him the Medal of Freedom, this country's highest civilian honor; and by the French, who accorded him the Medal of the Resistance and Croix de Guerre. His wife received the Legion of Honor.

The health of René had been undermined by the strain of the war years, and he died shortly after the return of his wife from Mauthausen in 1945.

Renault, Girard, and Dewavrin also survived the struggle

and merged again into peaceful occupations. Renault became an outstanding writer, much of his work dealing with
the war years in France. Dewavrin became a banker. Girard
married his secretary Denise Geninatti-Banck and took up
residence in Caen. All received various decorations for their
deeds.

After the liberation a man with a pump-handle jaw made
a significant statement to various former French resistance
leaders in Paris regarding "Century."

"I have something to say to you," American General
Omar N. Bradley declared. "I must inform you of the
gratitude of the American Army in regard to your network.
It was only after the reception in London of the plans of
the coastal defenses of the Channel area that we chose a
landing point and were able to make our arrangements. The
information that plan gave us was of such value that our
landing operation succeeded with a minimum loss of men
and material."

THE PHANTOMS IN THE FOREST

The four men were ragged and starving when the French
gamekeeper first met them in the forest on a midsummer's
day of 1940.

It was growing dark when they came stumbling through
the trees near the town of Loches, their clothes in tatters,
only vestiges of shoes on their feet. As soon as they spotted
the gamekeeper they halted uncertainly for a few seconds,
the whites of their eyes vivid in the dusk.

The gamekeeper, who had been walking rather briskly,
also came to a stop when he sighted the four men, his shot-
gun at the ready. There were many desperate men around
in fields and forests in that year.

"*Hey, vous autres, d'ou venez vous?* (Hey, you, where do
you come from?)" the gamekeeper exclaimed loudly.

The French words seemed to reassure the ragged quartet

standing about thirty yards away. They immediately replied in French that they were *soldats en fuite* (fleeing soldiers). Certain that the lone man was a Frenchman and seeing a friendly smile break out on his face, the four men immediately advanced and came to a standstill a few feet in front of him. Although almost unidentifiable due to dirt and tears, the clothes of the four were French army uniforms. This was unmistakable to the gamekeeper, a veteran of the French armies of World War I. He also knew from the men's physical appearance what kind of units they belonged to.

"Name of a dog, you fellows seem to be in bad shape," the gamekeeper said in a friendly fashion. "Come on, speak up."

"We are starving. Please get us some food, give us some help. We are almost finished," one of the four men replied. "We have been walking, running, hiding for days. We did not dare approach any house."

The men then told him that they had made their way southward from north of Tours, which is about fifty miles northwest of Loches, in central France.

Members of a regiment which had dissolved before the overwhelming German conquest, the quartet had decided to move southward in the general direction of the Mediterranean coast. They never had traveled during daylight hours. Fearful of capture by the Germans who were everywhere, they had subsisted on scraps of food found in empty barns or garbage pails. They had kept their trench knives but had been obliged to throw away all other arms as starvation weakened them.

"All right. I will do my best to help you," the gamekeeper said after listening to their story. "I have no love for the Boches* but they are all around here, especially in Loches itself, which is close to this forest. Rest here for the time being. I will be back in a short while with whatever food I can get, perhaps some wine."

* A derogatory word for Germans coined in World War I.

The soldiers thanked the gamekeeper warmly. Then they sank exhausted to the ground. The gamekeeper left them, heading for Loches.

The gamekeeper faced special problems, although incidents involving escaping French soldiers and civilians ready to help them were commonplace in those chaotic days.

All four soldiers were Negroes, Senegalese.

Senegalese troops had fought with French armies as regular regiments and divisions on many occasions, notably in World War I, always with outstanding valor. They had built up an exceptional reputation as cold steel fighters, virtuosos with trench knife and bayonet, especially in night operations.

The Germans displayed an almost traumatic fear of French Negro troops in both world wars. When the Nazis, to whom Negroes were sub-subhumans, first overran France they immediately made prisoner any colored men they met, making no distinction between those in uniform and civilians. The plight of the colored men in the debacle was fearsome. Due to their hue there was no question at all of any false identity papers to help them escape. The game was up once caught; either the execution squad or death in prison. None seized were ever seen again.

The gamekeeper returned to the forest that evening and brought the four men some bread and cheese, some fruit and milk, and a bottle of wine. He also brought some blankets and told them there was a stream nearby where they could get water. He warned them to lie low in thick shrubbery in that immediate area. Then promising to return the following day with more food, the gamekeeper headed for his home in Loches.

He kept his promise and the four men gradually regained their strength. As the days passed the gamekeeper's worries increased.

More and more German troops were concentrating in the Loches area. What if one or several soldiers should go strolling in the forest and spot the four men? Also the Senegalese had informed him they were determined to try to make their way south and somehow return to Africa. They had thus far evaded seizure but their chance of ever attaining the French Mediterranean coast was a remote one. There were masses of Germans between them and the coast.

There was a very small resistance cell in Loches at that time, just a handful of men who had secretly pledged themselves to do something against the Germans.

The gamekeeper knew one of these men and told him about his problem. He had not mentioned it to anyone else. For hours the two men discussed various possibilities. Despairing of a solution, they suddenly lit on a plan which might work for the time being. There was a kind of obelisk in the middle of the forest, called the Pyramid of St. Quentin. Near it were some fairly large fox warrens.

On the following day the gamekeeper and his companion contacted the Senegalese and led them to the obelisk area. Prowling around, the six men soon found a fox warren which would be suitable, provided it was enlarged.

Equipped with short spades provided by the gamekeeper, the Senegalese worked for almost two days enlarging the warren. This was extremely laborious but fortunately the woods were quite thick in that area. They could work by daylight, men taking turns as lookout while the others worked. Most of the time it involved one digger who had wormed head first into the warren. When he had dug enough, he wiggled his feet which were outside the warren's mouth and was dragged out. Then another man took his place.

Finally, the cave was about four feet high and just big enough for four men to lie down in with a fair degree of comfort. The entrance had been kept small and was well hidden by existing shrubbery and branch camouflage perfected by the Negroes. The walls of the hideout were plastered with mud to give them some degree of firmness. All traces of the work outside were removed. The cave, which was somewhat damp, was not exactly ideal for camping, but it was a much safer place than anywhere above ground in that area.

They stayed in the cave during the daytime and got their exercise by walking around in the forest at night. Each time they returned to their hideout the last man went in feet first. Before withdrawing into the hole, he carefully smoothed over the earth in front of the warren with a branch. It was arranged that the gamekeeper leave food daily at a certain place so that they could pick it up. All of the men kept their knives handy. When abroad they moved like American Indians on the warpath—warily, seldom bunched together, always scanning their surroundings. They found a tall tree from which a lookout could observe the town of Loches and its vicinity as night fell if they deemed this necessary.

Fortunately, the weather was warm with only occasional light rains. The life was not too bad for seasoned campaigners such as these men were. As the days passed, however, another enemy inevitably began to plague them—boredom, abetted by inaction. All had good cause to hate the Germans—they had seen friends shot by Germans, both black and white. They had a very clear idea of what Nazidom meant. All four began to wander farther afield at night—first toward the fringe of the forest, then into the outskirts of the town itself, where blackout regulations were in effect.

They prowled with a purpose. Its first evidence was a shocking one for the Germans in Loches: a sentry prone on a cobbled street who would never see the Fatherland again. His throat had been slit from ear to ear. He had been stripped of clothing down to his pants—boots, rifle, and ammunition missing. For several nights thereafter one or two Germans were killed in the same manner. As the killings progressed, clothing and arms were not pilfered. It was obvious that whoever was doing the killings had obtained enough arms and clothing for their needs.

Almost immediately the Germans suspected that this was,

in all probability, the work of the dread Senegalese who
had struck terror into Kaiser Wilhelm's men in World War I.
It was not a marked European custom to slit throats. The
Germans pounded from house to house, searching, questioning, but no one had seen any Negroes around. The gamekeeper and his resistance friend also were questioned but
shook their heads and replied like the others. If any French
person had seen dark shadows flitting through the streets
they kept their mouths shut.

The gamekeeper and the resistance man realized that this
could not keep up interminably. The baffled Germans would
soon seize some hostages in the town and execute them in
retaliation.

The resistance man contacted the quartet in the forest and
told them:

"This is all very well. Every Boche the less around here
is a fine thing but you should use some caution. When you
have bumped one off, cart him out of town and into the
forest and bury him. The Germans will then mark him
down as a deserter and this may lead them to believe the
whole bad dream is over and that whoever was doing it
had gone away."

The Senegalese expressed agreement with this advice.
They had buried the guns and ammunition in a hole near
the warren, deciding to use them only in a grave emergency. They decided the German helmets and jackets should
be worn as disguises. After refraining from any operations
for one night to lull the Germans, the dark-skinned warriors were on the *piste de guerre* (warpath) again.

For a few days no bodies with slit throats were found
in the streets but the list of deserters among the Germans
mounted. Since the recording of such defections was largely
a matter of paper work, the situation in Loches calmed
down.

But this reasonably happy state of affairs was not destined
to last overlong. At first the Senegalese did carry the bodies
away and bury them in the forest very carefully. After do-

ing this four or five times they got lazy. Carrying a body away was all right, but the wearisome process of burying it was too much. The Senegalese found a convenient gully in the forest, deep and far from any path, with a small stream running through the bottom of it. They began summarily dumping their ghastly burdens in this gully, covering the corpses lightly with boughs or handfuls of earth.

Even with this careless procedure the bodies might never have been discovered. However, the weather was quite hot. Soon a fierce stench began to drift out of the forest and into the town.

The gamekeeper and his friend realized that their forest friends had been neglectful. However, it was impossible for them to take any steps to have the bodies hurriedly buried. The Germans also had reacted quickly, figuring that the killers must still be around. The stench unquestionably came from the forest. Into the forest stomped a German platoon. After some scurrying around they found the bodies.

The infuriated Germans routed out a whole battalion of men and sent them on the double toward the forest. Machine-gun nests were set up at points where main roads entered or left the forest, which covered a considerable expanse. Then the men spread out and began searching it segment by segment, soldiers spaced about a yard apart. Sweating in the hot sunny weather, they combed the greenery from all sides, poking bayonets into shrubbery, stumbling into gullies, scanning the trees. They gave the ground a first going-over and then with Teutonic thoroughness did it all over again.

The Senegalese remained motionless in their hideout and prayed for luck. All their usual precautions had been taken. Twice German soldiers stopped and talked briefly right in front of the warren's screened opening. But the enemy detected nothing. The weary Germans clomped back to Loches that night as much in the dark as at the outset. Machine-gun nests were left on duty.

The gamekeeper warned his wards to stay close to home for a few days at least. This the fugitives did, but they could not be held in leash for long. It was easy to skirt around the German posts in the pitch dark, running stealthily on bare feet, the hue of their skin a perfect night camouflage.

German bodies again were found at dawn in Loches and also that of a sentry who had wandered too far from his machine-gun post at the forest's edge.

French jubilation over these night attacks soon was overshadowed by extreme anxiety. This could not go on. The Germans were being goaded to the point where they would snuff out the lives of innocent people, regardless of sex or age.

At this crucial juncture fate stepped in in the political sphere. The Germans and the Vichy government of Marshal Pétain agreed that the demarcation line between Nazi-occupied France and the southern, or so-called free zone, should run some twelve miles north of Loches, well beyond the forest.

As a result a general German withdrawal northward was carried out, many of the Germans, notably men in the ranks liable to night duty, inwardly very happy to leave a town where they were stalked by invisible death.

Although Loches and its environs were now under French rule which, servile to the Germans as it was, promised more leniency than German control, the gamekeeper and his resistance man decided to move very cautiously. Their secret was divulged to only a few trusted friends.

The Senegalese were informed of the favorable development and were provided with money, some spare clothing and plenty of food. Leaving their hideout, they bypassed the town and headed south, the way clear of German troops. Their status as French citizens and soldiers was certain to be respected in the Vichy zone, at least at that time. What eventually happened to them is not recorded.

As far as the population of Loches was concerned, it did

not hear of the forest phantoms until after the war. The gamekeeper and his immediate friends remained secretive just like foxes until their story could be safely divulged.

THE EYE OF SIVA AND OTHER EPISODES

Night without end

The battle-hardened American tank and infantry warriors of General George S. Patton first beheld No. 41,978 and the many other numbered humans near Weimar, Germany, in April 1945.

What the veterans saw jolted them, accustomed though they were to terrible scenes. None would ever quite forget the vision of the half-alive, the dying, and the dead. The thousands still living were skeletal wraiths, more like apparitions from the pits of hell than human beings.

The name of No. 41,978 was Jacques Lusseyran. He was a twenty-year-old Frenchman. His address at that time—the day of April 11—was Buchenwald concentration camp. Only the rapidity of the Allied advance toward the infamous camp had saved him and some 20,000 other inmates from wholesale massacre.

Lusseyran was a Parisian. He had much in common with another Frenchman then residing in Normandy, Arthur Poitevin. Their French ancestry dated way back. Both had been in the resistance, Lusseyran in the French capital and Poitevin in Normandy. Both were intellectuals with exceptional minds, their ability to remember facts, events, names, mathematical data, and other information bordering on the amazing. It is possible they also were jointly endowed with the mythical eye of Siva, the occult vision of Hindu religious beliefs.

German soldiers guarding the Atlantic Wall prior to the Allied invasion of Normandy had frequently seen Poitevin and the young boy who always accompanied him. They had no particular cause to remember the pair. Ostensibly both were harmless French strollers enjoying fresh sea air. Arrest and execution of both of them would have been immediate had the Germans been more curious. Poitevin and the boy, François Guerin, were part of Operation Century.

Like Lusseyran, Poitevin fought the Nazis effectively in a very special underground world. Here were no shadows, no sunlight, no moonlight.

The two Frenchmen were totally blind.

Lusseyran was originally chief of the Volunteers of Liberty in Paris, his birthplace. He had originated this movement which eventually had six hundred members, all young people, their ages ranging from fourteen to twenty. Their task was to disseminate clandestine newspapers, not only in the capital but elsewhere in France. In time Lusseyran, one of the earliest of the resistance men, became one of the top leaders, directing with a handful of other men the activities of one of the four or five biggest networks in France.

Lusseyran today is a professor of French literature at Western Reserve University in Cleveland, Ohio. He has lost none of the intellectual brilliance which in his youth marked him as one of France's most promising students, headed for the elite Ecole Normale Supérieure, the highest institution in the French educational system. A regulation regarding handicapped persons formulated by traitorous French government officials with the blessing of the Nazis prevented him from entering that school during the war years in Paris. This did not stop his mental or physical activity in any way whatsoever.

Lusseyran lost his vision in a school accident when he was eight. Accidentally pushed by a schoolmate, he fell and the arm of his glasses pierced his right eye. Despite prompt and skillful attention from a Paris specialist and devoted parental care, he lost sight first in the right eye and then in the left, which had also been injured.

"I was always running; the whole of my childhood was spent running," Lusseyran recalls in an autobiography recently published in this country entitled *And There Was*

Light. "Only I was not running to catch hold of something. That is a notion for grownups and not the notion of a child. I was running to meet everything that was visible, and everything that I could not see. I traveled from assurance to assurance, as though I were running a race in relays."

This statement refers to the period before he lost his sight. Some ten years after his accident the young Parisian was destined to dodge and run and hide from a ruthless enemy in his beloved City of Light for months on end.

It was not long after his accident before he had developed various senses to a fine pitch.

"As I walked along a country road bordered by trees I could point to each one of the trees by the road, even if they were not spaced by regular intervals," he wrote. "I knew whether the trees were straight and tall, carrying their branches as a body carries its head, or gathered into thickets and partly covering the ground around them . . . As with the sense of touch, what came to me from objects was pressure, but pressure of a kind so new to me that at first I didn't think of calling it by that name. When I became really attentive and did not oppose my own pressure to my surroundings, then trees and rocks came to me and printed their shape upon me like fingers leaving their impression in wax."

According to many traditions of the occult, man has a third eye, an inner eye, generally called the eye of Siva, located in the middle of his forehead.* This eye assertedly can be brought to life in certain conditions by special exercises. Researches undertaken by the French writer and member of the French Academy, Jules Romains, have demonstrated the existence of visual perception outside the retina, situated in certain nervous centers of the skin, par-

* Siva, or Shiva, the god of destruction, forms the Hindu Trinity with Vishnu and Brahma. Siva also is the deity of music, letters, and the dance.

ticularly the hands, the forehead, the nape of the neck, and the chest.

When the time came to act against the enemy, young Jacques had developed his various senses to the point where they veritably constituted an eye of Siva and would prove very valuable to the resistance as a whole.

He was studying at the Lycée when the Germans marched into Paris in the summer of 1940. At first, like many others he was lulled into a passive attitude by the overwhelming events and the initially correct attitude of the Germans. Early in 1941, however, Lusseyran decided that even blind as hc was he would do something against the Germans who were showing their tyrannical hand more harshly every day.

Jacques and several of his friends discussed the matter of doing some kind of resistance work. Then a number of other boys all in their teens were contacted, agreeing to meet at an apartment where one of the youngsters resided.

No definite line of action had been decided upon by any one. However, Lusseyran felt that the best thing to do at this time would be to help disseminate information and news which would counteract Nazi propaganda and the apathy which gripped a large portion of the population.

Some dozen boys had been expected at the meeting. Instead fifty-two turned up.

"When I heard the wave of voices climbing the narrow stairs of the apartment house, I had the foolish idea that someone had denounced us.

"But ten minutes later, when the fifty-two boys were sitting on their heels in the middle of the big room with the stained-glass windows, with all eyes turned in my direction, when suddenly they fell silent as I had never heard men fall silent, when one of them . . . said to me 'the chips are down, it's up to you to speak' then an unaccustomed radiance filled my head and my heart stopped beating out of rhythm. All at once I began to understand everything I had been seeking and not finding for the past weeks."

Perilous path

Lusseyran warned them that this was the beginning of a resistance movement, that there was no turning back. He pointed out that as long as people thought of them as kids they would not be suspected. It was decided that the movement would be called the Volunteers of Liberty. Its role would be passive at first, centering on enrollment of additional members. No arms, no sabotage attempts. Utmost secrecy must be observed. No more large gatherings in apartments as on that day. No more than three at a time must hold meetings, and these only to tackle grave emergencies.

A central committee consisting of Lusseyran and several other youngsters, none older than twenty, was formed to guide the network's strategy. The blind leader agreed to be in sole charge of recruiting for the first few months.

"They claimed I had 'the sense of human beings,'" he wrote in his memoirs. "In my first encounters (in the weeks following the meeting) I had made no mistakes (sanctioning new enrolees). Besides, I would hear more acutely and pay better attention. People could not easily deceive me. I should not forget names or places, addresses or telephone numbers. Every week I would report on the outlook without resorting to scraps of paper or lists. Anything written down, even in code, was a risk that none of us had the right to run."

In less than a year the Volunteers for Liberty counted six hundred boy members. One by one they first had been screened by one of the original fifty-two. Then they were sent to the blind leader at his home in an apartment in the Boulevard Port-Royal where he lived with his parents who were "in the know."

Security was strict—all the boys knew that danger was everywhere, that even a casual word of gossip dropped by some neighbor might reach the ears of the Germans. Each new recruit had to arrive within five minutes of the ap-

pointed hour. He had to climb the main stairway to the
fourth floor and give two short rings and one long on the
bell. If an aspiring recruit did not fully adhere to these
conditions Lusseyran had the option of just not answering
his apartment door or letting the bellringer in and talking
about nothing important.

The leader of the Volunteers realized soon that it was of
paramount importance to provide the French people with
news, real news, not the distorted, doctored news in regular
French papers. Listening to the British Broadcasting Company programs was forbidden by the Nazis. Dissemination
of foreign newspapers which might give the lie to Nazi reports had been choked off.

"Our first job was to bring out a newspaper—a paper,
or if that should be beyond our means at the start, a loose-
leaf news bulletin, one we could circulate in secret from
hand to hand," Lusseyran recalls.

Trusted members were promptly assigned to listen regularly to British and Swiss radio programs and to make reports to the Central Committee of executions, troop movements, arrests, deportations, and the like.

Somewhat like the Baker Street Irregulars of Sherlock
Holmes, these boys of Paris as time passed became, among
other things, a widespread information network.

"Young as we were, we could easily go all over, pretend
to be playing games, or making foolish talk, wander around
whistling with our hands in our pockets, outside factories,
near barracks or German convoys, hang about kitchens and
on sidewalks, climb over walls. Everything would be on our
side, even help from girls if there happened to be any on
the spot."

At first the Volunteers helped disseminate two news-
sheets put out by another network entitled La France Continue and Resistance. Then it succeeded in putting out its
own news bulletin, a crude, mimeographed affair. But it contained valid news. News writing was done by Lusseyran
and other students acting as editors. Mimeographing was

done in secret, at one time in an unoccupied padded cell in St. Anne's Psychiatric Hospital where demented women were cared for. A young doctor who practiced at the hospital had arranged for the use of this cell after a talk with Lusseyran. Since the Nazis controlled sale of paper, various boys had to steal it in a series of raids.

The bulletin was run off at fairly regular intervals and then slipped under doors, dropped in stores, offices, and schools, and in buses and subways by hundreds of boys. Frequently the distributors were operating within full eyeshot of German soldiers, officers, or police.

Publication of the bulletin kept the volunteers busy until the fall of 1942. Then Lusseyran met the leader of a larger resistance movement, grouping mostly adults, and called Défense de la France. It was promptly decided that the Volunteers should merge with it, its youngsters an enormous asset in distribution of that network's paper, *Défense de la France.*

This was a real newspaper with 10,000 copies run off monthly. The Défense movement had a print shop manned by amateurs turned professional. It had presses, paper, arms and machine guns, ten underground branches in Paris, several small trucks disguised as delivery wagons, a factory for counterfeit papers which could produce 2500 fake identity cards a month, and a radio transmitter which maintained contact with de Gaulle's government in London. It extended beyond Paris, having supporters in Seine-et-Oise and other areas.

The youngsters of Lusseyran's group ensured wider distribution of this paper, all of them skilled and well-organized in this work, their youthfulness always an excellent camouflage, their energy boundless. Other papers were being published by networks with which DF had some contact. The boys also helped distribute these from time to time. They included *Résistance, Combat, Libération* and *Franc-Tireur* (*Franc-Tireur* means a guerrilla or civilian sharpshooter in French).

Early in 1943 the circulation of *Défense de la France*
jumped to 20,000 copies.

"The paper's chief task was the awakening of conscience,"
Lusseyran points out. ". . . In February, 1943, for instance,
we said what no one in Europe was saying at the time,
specifically that the Nazi army had just fallen into a trap
at Stalingrad and that the future course of the war was
about to be reversed in the ruins of that city."

The paper also gave advice on passive resistance and re-
morselessly aired details on *Gestapo* torturing of prisoners
and the systematic extermination of Jews, developments
which the Nazis, of course, strove to keep secret.

The circulation of *Défense de la France*, issued twice a
month, jumped by leaps and bounds as the winter and spring
months turned into the summer of 1943. By July 14 it
totaled 250,000, being distributed not only in Paris but
throughout France. The number of persons responsible for
its distribution had risen to five thousand, including the six
hundred Volunteers of Liberty as well as many young girls.

During this period Lusseyran and other scholars continued
their studies, dividing their time between this and resistance
activity. All realized, however, that the larger an underground organization became, the greater danger for its
members.

Not only were the *Gestapo* and the *Abwehr* on the hunt,
but also the loathsome Milice, police units composed of
French Nazis and any other riffraff that could be enrolled.

These bands were at times more dangerous to the resistance than any German forces. Their speciality was to
infiltrate the ranks of the underground posing as patriotic
Frenchman. Again and again they succeeded in doing so
with grave results for the movement involved.

The living dead

In March one of the secret print shops where copies of the
newspaper were run off had to be moved quickly for it
was being shadowed by the *Gestapo*.

Five boys acted as decoys, leading an equal number of German agents in long and futile hunts in five different directions. The boys knew the tricks: how to enter the front door of a store and rush out through the service entrance, how to elude pursuers in subways and in narrow twisting streets. While the hunt was on—involving the *Gestapo* men in that area at the moment—other resistance men moved all the machinery to another secret point in vans marked OPTICAL INSTRUMENTS. FRAGILE. NATIONAL METEOROLOGICAL OBSERVATORY.

In May the leaders of DF had to make a grave decision. The network badly needed to coordinate distribution in the northern area of France. The job had to be confided to a man named Elio who had recently applied for membership.

His credentials were good. He was twenty-five, a medical student of Paris, endorsed by a highly reliable group leader in the College of Medicine. He had served faithfully in another resistance outfit for a year.

Lusseyran was suspicious of him from the first, but for once he hesitated.

"He had appeared on his own at my apartment without being summoned," Lusseyran recalls. "At once all my senses were on the alert. Then something unusual took place. This man threw my mechanism out of gear; my inner needle kept oscillating, not settling either on the 'yes' or the 'no.' Elio spoke in a low voice, too low. His voice was like his handshake (which Lusseyran had deemed too heavy). It lacked clarity and straightforwardness."

In spite of Lusseyran's suspicions, Elio was sent to the north in a position of trust since he knew the area very well.

This was the beginning of the end of resistance for Lusseyran and many of his friends. Elio was an infiltrator working for the Germans. To lull suspicions of the resistance he performed excellently in the city of Lille during June and early July.

On July 19 at about 5:00 A.M. there came the dreaded

knock on the door of the Lusseyran apartment. There were
six Germans—two officers and four soldiers. They took
Jacques away but did not manhandle him. Before they left
they ransacked his room, scattering five or six thousand
sheets of Braille on the floor. Apparently this material made
no sense to them. They found no documents. All vital information was in Jacques' mind, including hundreds of
memorized Paris telephone numbers.

For days Jacques was questioned at *Gestapo* headquarters
or left solitary in a cell. He was not tortured but one
angry SS officer lifted him and threw him violently against
a wall on two occasions. The Germans had a fifty-page
dossier on him compiled, as Lusseyran learned later, by
Elio. He had also provided them with the names of countless other persons in the DF movement.

Weeks and months of imprisonment in the terrible Fresnes
prison followed. He was not permitted to communicate with
his parents. In January, 1944, he was herded into the prison
camp at Compiègne, joining some ten thousand other resistance men slated for deportation to German concentration camps. Some of his friends in DF were among them.

On a bitterly cold morning Lusseyran and ninety-four
other men were sealed into one of those freight cars which
became so familiar to American soldiers in World War I.
It was labeled QUARANTE HOMMES. HUIT CHEVAUX, which
meant it could transport either forty men or eight horses.
Some two thousand other Frenchmen were also in that day's
convoy. The German's, of course, ignored the capacity desig-
nation. The prisoners were packed in to the point where
there was no room to lie down. There was no food, no water.

The train convoy was headed for Buchenwald.

Lusseyran amazingly continued to function as an underground newsman in the camp itself. Every day at specified
times the SS guards would broadcast news—German news.
After the Allied invasion of June, 1944, the German military
announcements became increasingly vague. It was Lusseyran's job to memorize the announcements and analyze them

in such a manner that actual developments would be revealed.

"When we came to the middle of August, 1944, the name of Paris never appeared in the bulletins," Lusseyran writes. "No defeat, no lost city was ever mentioned, you had to fill in the gaps without making any mistakes. Still, I announced the fall of Paris on August 26, and that was neither ahead of time nor behind it."

Lusseyran made his announcements verbally, going from barracks to barracks. He spoke in French and German. In the camp were Czechs, Russians, and prisoners of other nationalities who understood him and could translate the news into the language of their countries.

In addition, some prisoners had actually built in secret a radio transmitting and receiving set which they operated in a cellar. This news also was disseminated by Lusseyran but more cautiously lest it should lead to discovery of the set.

When the Americans stabbed into the Weimar area in April, 1945, the Germans offered the 100,000-odd inmates two alternatives: stay in the camp at their own risk or head eastward under SS guard.

Eighty thousand prisoners, numbed by months of horror, alarmed by the thunder of guns nearby, decided to take their chances with the SS and departed under heavy guard. Lusseyran and 20,000 other inmates decided to stay.

A big SS contingent remained behind. The Nazi thugs had no intention of sparing the 20,000. All food stores had been poisoned. At 1:30 P.M., April 11, orders were issued over the loudspeakers to exterminate all survivors.

They did not know Patton, however. The general guessed that any delay might mean the death of thousands. He mounted a swift enveloping attack in the direction of Buchenwald, aided by information transmitted by the secret radio set in the camp. The SS men about to start the extermination, were forced to flee or surrender. The other 80,000 prisoners were killed en masse by machine-gun fire

of the SS a few days later some sixty miles southeast of Buchenwald.

In a few weeks Lusseyran was returned to Paris, again a
city of light and freedom. His cherished *Défense de la
France* never was completely knocked out by the Germans.
Its membership increasing daily in spite of the 1943 blows,
it fought the good fight to the end, publishing its militant
paper regularly.

The sightless spy

"Ah, it is good to smell the salt, feel the sun and wind on
your cheeks, François," the blond man in the shabby gray
suit said, tapping his cane on the ground. "And the steady
swoosh of the waves. The waves are like music to me. Now
let us concentrate again. What do you see, François, *mon
ami*, that might be interesting?"

The dark-haired, handsome boy, holding the man by the
arm, replied:

"I can see a casemate. It is right near us, within good eyeshot. It's a big one and I can see at least one large gun.
My guess is that it's about 150 feet from here and about a
thousand paces from the shoreline. The strongpoint has been
built on a chalk foundation, I think."

"Very good, François, and now tell me in what direction
the gun is pointed," the man asked.

"Toward the northwest at present," the boy replied.

Giving the man's arm a gentle nudge, the boy added:

"Now we are turning back toward Port-en-Bessein, Arthur. I am going to start counting our paces so that we can
figure approximately the distance between the main jetty and
the casemate. I know you will remember everything as usual.
I really have come to think that you see better than I do.
There are some Germans in uniform about a hundred yards
away but they are busy talking as usual and have only fa-
vored us with fleeting glances."

Walking slowly, the boy counting his steps carefully, the

pair strolled slowly along the breakwater toward the central part of the tiny Normandy coastal town, some 20 miles northwest of Caen. Their stroll completed, the boy carefully informed his companion of the calculations he had made. Then the two walked toward a bicycle with a small side-car attached to it. The man clambered into the side-car and the boy mounted the cycle. Pedalling steadily he headed the machine for the town of Bayeux, some ten miles inland, where both resided.

For both the man and the boy this trip was almost a daily occurrence in the late summer months of 1942. The Germans paid little attention to them—obviously a blind man being led on a stroll by a young friend. They never did anything suspicious like jotting down notes, using binoculars or taking photographs. They never asked questions. When they passed close to a German they usually uttered a polite "Bonjour" and continued on their stroll. The Germans never guessed what was the main purpose of their walks or what they talked about. None knew that the man had a fabulous memory for facts and figures.

Both man and boy were agents of Operation Century. They were garnering valuable data on the Atlantic Wall defenses in the Port-en-Bessein area, right in the middle of beaches which eventually would be named Omaha and Gold.

The man was blind Arthur Poitevin, a music teacher. The Poitevins were on William the Conqueror's ships when they sailed from Normandy to conquer Saxon England in 1066 A.D.

The boy was François Guerin, a student of Bayeux, a handsome sixteen-year-old with blue eyes and curly black hair, a good soccer player and an excellent swimmer.

Drawn together by mutual intellectual interests, particularly music, they had become fast friends even before the war started. Both had agreed to work for Century in the spring of 1942. By the summer of that year Century badly needed detailed information about the Atlantic Wall in the Port-en-Bessein sector. From the seaward side agents in fishing or other boats had been able to provide some general information but this was not enough. The problem was how to get close enough to the fortifications in the land area to be able to record details for which London was clamoring. Repeated strolls by adult agents, singly or in pairs, could prove dangerous. In addition, there was the problem of memorizing accurately all kinds of facts regarding the fortifications. Something had to be evolved which would lull all German suspicions.

One plan after another was rejected when François came up with an idea at a Century meeting. He and Arthur could do it. His youth and the fact that his companion was blind undoubtedly would shield them from sharp investigation. His cycle with side-car would come in handy in the whole business, François pointed out.

The plan was approved and worked excellently. Their strolls centered mainly on the harbor breakwater at Port-en-Bessein. Possibly through some compassion for a blind man, German guards frequently let them extend their coastal walks through areas where other persons would have been questioned and ordered to go back to the town.

Day after day Poitevin acted as a sort of human IBM machine which stored away complex information fed to it by Guerin—estimated distances of one casemate from the other, descriptions of types of guns, terrain undulations, location of barbed wire and guard posts, progress of construction work. Anything the boy could see which he deemed important was quietly conveyed to Poitevin, frequently in full view of German guards or soldiers.

At night in his studio in Bayeux, Poitevin effortlessly and accurately recapitulated all the information obtained in the day's work. Guerin wrote this down in invisible ink on cigarette paper. From the studio the information was funneled to Caen, from where it eventually reached London.

Neither Poitevin or Guerin was arrested although they were active in various ways in the Normandy resistance until the Nazis fled eastward. The information they provided proved very valuable to British forces when they stormed ashore at Port-en-Bessein in 1944.

Captivating lady

Women, both foreign and French, played important roles in the resistance in that country although the preceding stories do not deal with their roles in detail.

Great numbers were eventually arrested, tortured, and shot or jailed in fearful prisons in France or in German concentration camps. The Germans had a special place for women prisoners, Ravensbruck concentration camp. It was one of the most infamous of all the camps. Few women survived Ravensbruck.

In France there were numerous Englishwomen who did outstanding work. Some were residents, others were visitors, and still others were secretly sent in as special agents by parachute, fishing boat, and even by submarine.

One of the most extraordinary of these women was beautiful, blond Roxane Pitt. Roxane's father was English, her mother the daughter of the Marquis of Mendoza, an enormously wealthy Spanish grandee who was Jewish.

Roxane was living in Paris when the Nazis came. Speaking French and an ardent Francophile, Roxane got drawn into resistance work of various types and eventually became a full-fledged British spy in that country and later in Italy.

In one phase of her work in Paris, Roxane, who had studied for the stage, was operating in the cast of the *Folies Bergères*. This provided her with a working permit to back false identity papers. German officers frequently invited the actresses to cocktail parties. At one time she attended a gala reception for Field Marshal von Witzleben, one of Hitler's top commanders and one who had strongly urged the building of an Atlantic Wall. She had been told to obtain any information she could about rumors that Germany and Italy were planning a joint attack against Spain. It was suspected that Witzleben was headed for an important conference with Italian commanders in the Vichy zone on this matter.

Roxane was introduced to the Marshal and proved very attractive to him. The Marshal knew French fairly well and an animated exchange developed. Roxane imitated a southern French accent and told him she was deeply worried about the situation of her family in the south. Deftly she implied that she would not be averse to taking a trip with him in his car if he was planning to go southward in following days.

His answer "I can't go this week, later perhaps" convinced Roxane that some important conference was on, that the Marshal did not consider this a time for gay jaunts with pretty ladies.

British Intelligence believed that if he went to Vichy and stayed there something big was afoot regarding Spain. If he returned it would be an indication that the plan had been shelved. Another agent kept close watch on Witzleben and ascertained he had left for the Vichy zone the next day. Some ten days later Roxane was at a party attended by an aide-de-camp of Witzleben and he told her that the Marshal had indicated he would help her get south to her family.

"His Excellency is in Paris," the aide-de-camp replied. "He is too busy to take you down south yet; but don't lose hope, the war will soon be over."

As a result of this probing, British Intelligence concluded that plans regarding Spain were definitely off—which eventually proved correct.

Roxane had many other exciting adventures not only in France but in Italy where she was parachuted behind enemy lines to do undercover work. She survived the conflict and returned to England after the Allied victory in Europe, one of those agents whom the Germans and Italians never caught.

Another heroine of the underground was an American woman named Etta Shiber, who spoke French fluently and had visited France frequently prior to the war with her husband.

When her husband died shortly before the outbreak of
hostilities, she went to stay with a Frenchwoman known as
Kitty Beaurépos in Paris. After the arrival of the Germans
she and her friend became involved in the dangerous business of aiding the flight of stranded Allied soldiers and airmen.

One of their principal aides was a Catholic priest named
Father Christian who temporarily hid escapees in a warehouse room in his church near Paris. In one instance the
two women engineered a spectacular escape of a Briton from
a prison near Paris. The Briton, who was still suffering from
wounds, was literally stuffed into the luggage compartment
of their small car. Then the two women drove back to their
apartment in Paris, narrowly missing searches by Germans.

Both women finally were captured and were shuttled from
one prison to another in France. They were never together
during imprisonment.

The American woman might very well have been executed but for the one fortuitous occurrence. In 1938 the
American FBI had arrested the hairdresser of the luxury passenger liner, *Bremen*, on suspicion she was a member of a
dangerous German spy ring in the United States. She was a
blowzy red-haired woman with a coarse face, named Johanna Hoffman.

The Germans thought Johanna quite a superdame and
wanted her back under the swastika. In 1942 an agreement
was reached through various channels to have the redhead
exchanged for Mrs. Shiber.

Mrs. Shiber returned to the United States via Spain and
died in this country a few years ago. As far as is known,
she was the only American woman who became fully involved in the French resistance and endured imprisonment
as a result. In a book she wrote about her experiences—published during the war in this country—she never divulged
the true name of Kitty. The book indicated that Kitty was
executed but that Father Christian survived.

The one-eyed fugitive

The plane, coming from London, droned steadily through the skies of France on a clear midsummer night of 1943 and headed for the town of Moulins, about 170 miles south of Paris.

When the plane reached the vicinity of Moulins it circled over a large field. A stocky young Frenchman in parachutist's garb dove earthward from a hatchway. The plane then headed back for the English Channel as the Frenchman's parachute opened and billowed earthward, a shifting blob in the darkness.

The Frenchman's name was Jacques, a London-trained agent, assigned to radio transmission.* He landed successfully without being detected and hid his parachute. Having completed his first drop in enemy-held territory, Jacques then proceeded furtively on foot to a nearby village to contact French underground cells, according to detailed instructions given him in London.

At that time Jacques had both his eyes—his vision exceptionally good. He would not enjoy this physical asset for long. A savage ordeal awaited him involving one of the most extraordinary escapes in the annals of underground warfare.

The Frenchman began transmitting information to London the next day. This continued for three weeks until some informer tipped off the Germans. Jacques was seized and turned over to the *Gestapo* at Clermont-Ferrand, farther south.

The *Gestapo* gave him a full treatment, determined to make him divulge code secrets. There was no chance for Jacques to use his cyanide pill—it had been immediately seized by the Germans when he was captured.

Jacques proved a very stubborn captive. His lips remained sealed in spite of brutal beatings. Infuriated, the Germans

---

* As in many other stories about the resistance, it is impossible at this date to trace the real names of persons involved.

then gouged out his right eye with a steel bar. This operation completed, the Germans then left the second-story
room where the interrogation took place and went downstairs to have lunch.

Jacques had been handcuffed to a chair. Although in
agony, he was conscious. By twisting and turning he managed to break the chair. Still handcuffed he clambered
through a window and fell onto a small roof below, making
considerable noise. Desperate, he got off the roof and ran
along the top of a wall. He jumped off the wall into a street
below. The torturers had heard him.

In landing, the Frenchman had stumbled and fallen to his
knees. He rose and ran up the street, and took the first turning to the right. The Germans were now in full cry, having
spotted him as he rose from his fall. They were coming up
fast behind him. Turning the corner Jacques saw a Frenchman walking toward him who was wearing a hat.

"Don't say anything," he said hurriedly. Raising his handcuffed hands he removed the man's hat, put it on his own
head and continued on his way as slowly as was advisable.

When the Germans rounded the corner they saw two men,
one walking toward them and another already at some distance away with a hat on. Ignoring a second turn, Jacques
continued walking, keeping his handcuffed hands in front of
him. The Germans came on and, apparently convinced that
the man with the hat was not Jacques, plunged around the
second turn. At the end of that street a hatless man was
walking rather quickly, away from them. They went after
him. By the time they ascertained he was nobody they
wanted, their real quarry had vanished in a side street and
hidden himself in a backyard.

At nightfall, Jacques succeeded in stealthily leaving the
town and hid in nearby woods that night, dozing off occasionally in spite of his pain.

The next day he continued his journey, shunning people,
houses, roads, eating whatever vegetables or fruit he could
obtain. He had gone some twenty miles with periods of rest

when he realized that he must get help, even though there always was the risk of contacting some treacherous person.

Eventually he met a blacksmith bicycling along a road and begged him for aid. The blacksmith was a patriotic Frenchman and brought him to his smithy where he broke the handcuffs. Then he and his wife hid him in their home. A doctor was summoned who was trustworthy and gave him medical attention, promising to return in a few days. Lovingly cared for by the couple, Jacques felt strong enough to move again in about two weeks.

He joined a local Maquis band, through which he contacted London and was instructed that he must get back to England. Although unwilling to do so, Jacques had to obey and got back to London via Spain after weeks of journeying.

Although his superiors did not favor his pleas to return to France, the one-eyed man finally obtained permission. Eight months after his escape from the *Gestapo* he was back in France. There he resumed his radio transmitting activities. He was not captured again.

Jacques had been trained for his job by the British Special Operations Executive, sometimes referred to as Subversive Operations Executive. The French resistance as well as underground movements in other countries received their most substantial and protracted outside help from this extraordinary, hush-hush organization.

Established shortly after the outbreak of the war, SOE gradually developed into what undoubtedly was the most efficient organization of its type ever created. Its broad task was to aid underground operations in every way possible. The whole idea was something new—no organization quite identical had ever been created in wartime.

SOE was subdivided into various departments, each devoted to some particular country, staffed by experts. The organization, with its headquarters in London, operated most of the time in liaison with governments-in-exile and the Free French.

It selected and trained a large number of special agents, both women and men. Some were Britons with linguistic knowledge and other qualifications making them suitable for work in a particular country. The majority chosen, however, were natives of a particular country who either had escaped or were abroad at the time the Germans poured in.

All men selected for this secret work went through intensive training in England and Scotland designed to ready them for any kind of armed or other action. The curriculum included some of the following:

Jiu-jitsu and other forms of self-defense or aggression using hands, feet and body weight.

Silent killings with knives or other sharp-edged weapons.

Radio transmission including Morse code and various secret codes.

Parachute jumping by day and by night.

Methods of effecting a quick disguise, such as stuffing cotton in mouths to change facial contours.

The handling of all types of hand arms, including German rifles, pistols, submachine guns and machine guns.

These were some of the main facets of the training. When they were ready to go, clothing worn by agents was of the type usually seen at that time in the country involved, depending on what status they would assume. The same applied to shoes. Such minor details as the type of cigarettes they carried were not overlooked. Anyone found smoking British or American cigarettes in an occupied country would be in danger—the Germans were very watchful in this matter.

Planes of various types were used for drops of parachutists and supplies, the latter in specially developed containers. Such drops usually were made at night in areas agreed upon in prior exchanges of information with underground personnel in the country itself. Usually underground operators were waiting for the plane on the ground, signaling with flashlights to indicate just where it should land.

A rather slow-moving British plane called a Lysander was extensively used, especially in France, for such missions. The Lysander became something of a byword in the underground warfare, although it was nothing spectacular as a plane. This two-seater, propeller-driven plane had a top speed of 206 miles an hour at sea level under favorable conditions. It had one great advantage in this type of work. Its motor was not too noisy, it was very maneuverable and dependable, and it could land anywhere with relative ease and take-off in a limited area.

In the latter half of the war the American OSS became increasingly active in aiding the underground. In January 1944 it merged with SOE to form Special Forces Headquarters. The Americans dropped large quantities of arms and supplies in France and elsewhere and sent some 275 American and French agents into France alone. A number of Americans joined the Maquis and participated in dangerous sabotage operations and in stiff fighting against the Germans.

Large numbers of agents were captured, tortured, and killed in spite of the most elaborate preparations and precautions. On various occasions they were captured immediately, having been injured and incapacitated by a faulty landing or because they dropped through some mistake in the wrong area.

The Maquis strikes

NOTICE TO ALL FRENCHMEN

1. MEN needed in the Maquis to fight. They will live badly and dangerously. Food will be scarce. They will be completely separated from their families until the end of the war. Violators of this rule of isolation will

be punished. No pay will be guaranteed. Efforts will be made to help their families, but no promises can be given. All correspondence (letter writing) is forbidden.

2. EQUIPMENT TO BRING: Two shirts, two pairs of drawers, a woollen undershirt, two pairs of woollen socks, a scarf, a pullover, a woollen blanket, an extra pair of shoes, laces, needle and thread, trouser buttons, safety pins, soap, canteen, mess kit, knife, fork and spoon, metal cup, pocket lamp, compass, firearm if possible, a sleeping bag if you can get one. Wear a warm suit, a beret, a raincoat, a good pair of hobnailed shoes.

3. COME with identity papers, even if forged, but in perfect legal order. Bring your labor card for crossing police barriers, your ration card and food tickets. These latter are essential.

These were the instructions contained in leaflets distributed by the underground in France to warn aspirant Maquis of what faced them and what preparations were advisable on their part.

Naturally not all men could meet all the requirements, notably in regard to clothing, arms, and shoes. Many teenagers and older men took to the hills in desperate hurry and had to be supplied with whatever arms and equipment could be spared. Once enrolled, men and women—a large number of women joined the Maquis—were under very stern military regulations. Loss of weapons of any type could be followed by drum-head court-martial and even execution. If a traitor was found in the ranks and caught, death came swiftly.

The Maquis forces, eventually known as the French Forces of the Interior (FFI), were the organized combat arm of the resistance, secret armies operating in various areas. These forces could range from small formations of twenty men or less to groupings of thousands of men.

It developed into the most hard-hitting, most powerful, behind-the-lines fighting force in any occupied country.

Maquisard garb usually was as varied as the personalities of those enrolled, most frequently rather shabby but practical civilian attire, sometimes worn but distinguishable military uniforms. The most popular headgear was the traditional French beret, usually blue or black in color.

Virtually all of them were young, under thirty. There were recorded instances, however, of relatively old persons in the ranks, one a woman of seventy-odd years. She was armed and fought in several engagements.

Their operations can best be compared to the warring methods of American Indians. They had their own French term for their tactics: *"Surprise, mitraillage, évanouissement* (Surprise, blast of fire, disappearance)."

They struck everywhere, rather poorly armed in the very beginning, well armed in the later phase of France's resistance battle. Their total casualties were heavy but those suffered by the Germans during their attacks were much greater. One of their particularly stirring feats was the seizure of the town of Oyonnax, in southeastern France, on Armistice Day, November 11, 1943. The town, which has a population of about 12,000, was held for a full day and then the Maquisards withdrew in orderly fashion, leaving numerous German casualties in their wake.

Detailed eyewitness accounts of Maquis attacks were transmitted to London by radio or other means. Following is one such account, a night attack against the important Schneider du Creusot plant manufacturing arms and other matériels. The plant, then German-controlled, is located in the southeastern Jura region, mountainous terrain not far from Oyonnax and close to the Swiss border. It was reported by one of the attackers, who struck at night.

"After crossing the Saône River, we hid in a gully bordering the river, at 1500 meters from the plant (a meter is 39.37 inches). We prepare out material. At 21 hours (9:00 P.M.) we begin to approach our target, crawling or moving quickly in crouched positions.

"Reaching the big pylon (electric tower) nearest to us we place our explosives at its base. Then we continue our advance and reach various exit gates (these were presumably gates in wire fencing or walls surrounding the big plant). Explosives are placed here also. At 21:30 hours this preparatory action has been completed.

"Now we advance toward the plant itself, which is guarded by two Germans and 20 gendarmes (the latter probably members of the hated Milice). We are bothered by the strong searchlight playing on the one spot where we can enter the plant. Avoiding this light area, we cross a road on our stomachs in the darkness, undetected by two nearby gendarmes. Successfully negotiating a 1500-volt defensive electric wiring in our path, we reach the main plant area and place our delayed action bombs at points which had been carefully planned in advance. Then we leave silently and cautiously by the same way we had come. We had not been seen.

"At 12:45, Gate C exploded with a terrific bang. Five minutes later magnificent fireworks, blast after blast. Searchlights go on everywhere. The explosions cause panic among the gendarmes, the Boches and whatever plant personnel is around. Fires rage and ignite fuel tanks. Huge clouds of smoke envelop the plant, coiling skyward to a formidable height. Twenty-five heavy explosions occur up to 3:15 A.M."

The attack, it was established later, halted work in the plant for six months. All electrical transformers in the plant were knocked out, fuel supplies burned, various types of machinery destroyed, and high tension wires wrecked. These wires daily carried an enormous quantity of electric current, 80 per cent of it for the Reich and 20 per cent for the operation of the plant.

Not a single Maquisard was wounded. The casualties in the plant, if any, were not ascertained.

Information reaching the Free French disclosed countless attacks which were obviously the work of the Maquis in many areas. Following are some examples which occurred also in the fall of 1943.

• A train bearing German soldiers on leave derailed between Porquigny and Mangest. One hundred killed, some 250 wounded.

• Maquisards derailed a train on the Besançon-Belfort line. Fifty-two German soldiers on leave killed, 80 wounded.

• At Le Mans six automobiles, 25 motorcycles, and seven side-cars being transported on three railway cars were wrecked by bomb blasts.

• Maquisards placed explosives in a large shipment of mines heading for Italy. The mines were completely destroyed in a terrible blast.

• A train transporting 1,200,000 liters of gasoline (about 300,000 gallons) was derailed at Varennes.

GALLIC THERMOPYLAE

Not far from the ancient university city of Grenoble, in France's southeastern mountain zone, is a high, forbidding mountain plateau known as the Vercors.

What happened there in the summer of 1944 after the Allied landings in Normandy far to the northwest has made the plateau an immortal name in French history. Here the Maquisards fought their Thermopylae.

A graphic eyewitness account of what happened on the plateau was penned by one of the survivors, Michel Prévost. Michel was a very young Maquisard. He was only sixteen years old.

The plateau in its whole circumference can only be reached by eight paths, all of them difficult even to experienced mountaineers.

Bands of Maquisards had been using the plateau as a base before 1944 but it only became of major importance after the Allied landings in June of that year.

Heeding orders from London, French resistance leaders ordered large numbers of Maquisards to converge on the plateau and transform it into a bastion. Such a bastion would harass the Germans when Allied forces carried out scheduled landings in the south of France.

Part of the top area of the plateau is flat. The French promptly smoothed it over so that Allied planes could land on it.

The Germans, following up an indecisive attack in early June, went all out against the plateau in mid-July with two full infantry divisions, backed by artillery. The French held throughout that day and the next in bitter fighting. Barring a few bazookas and mortars they had no artillery.

During the night of the nineteenth the French appealed by radio for Allied aerial support, especially paratroops who could land on the plateau from gliders towed by warplanes or drop to their aid by parachute.

Michel and his father, Jean Prévost, a promising young French writer, were on the plateau at the time. Both were residents of Veiron, a village on a plain close to the Vercors.

The elder Prévost had been in the Grenoble resistance movement from the beginning, acting most of the time as one of the liaison couriers between the Grenoble area and Paris, most of his assignments involving bicycling from one point to another.

"In the spring of 1944 we left Veiron and went to live on the plateau itself," Michel recalled in his account. "When the Allies landed in Normandy, activity redoubled on our plateau. My father and his bicycle were absent for days at a time; groups of Maquisards would swoop in lightning-like raids across the valley. I sat glued to my radio fretting at the lack of sensational news.

"On June 9, a young man came to the house and leaned his bicycle against the steps. He asked for Captain Goderville, which was my father's Maquis name. He had brought my father the mobilization order for the Vercors Maquis." (These probably were resistance mobilization orders for all

Maquisards in the Grenoble area to concentrate on the plateau.)

"My father wasted no time. He took his knapsack and his uniform and I brought him two revolvers which had been stuffed into an old pair of boots and hidden under a pile of rocks in the garden. He stuffed his uniform and guns into his knapsack and rode off on his bicycle as if he were setting out on an accustomed errand. I was to meet him in the morning.

"At 2:00 A.M. I left on foot for the Goule Noir bridge. A liaison agent met me and drove me to the farmhouse where the Goderville company, my father's, was stationed. The outbuildings were swarming with Maquisards, busy cleaning and loading their arms. I climbed into the loft of the barn where men were sleeping in the hay. Over in the corner, officers were bending over a map. I went over and said, 'Hello, Dad.'

"'I'm glad you got here, son,' he answered. He and the men with him smiled at me briefly and went back to their maps.

"A little later, before dawn, we left for St. Nizier. Ordered to establish our defense line there, our mission was to keep the Germans off that part of the plateau. We were told to expect reinforcements by parachute. While the officers reconnoitered and organized outposts, I stayed behind in the village to watch the men set up their machine guns. By evening, we were all in our positions. My father and I were with some other men in a hayloft and he said to me: 'It's a funny thing to have my son as a comrade-in-arms.'

"Three days later the Germans attacked us. With my father, I watched small knots of men in gray-green climb up the steep slopes toward our position. Since I was assigned the job of stretcher bearer, my father told me to take my stretcher behind the Guillet house and added: 'Don't take the ridge road. Take the one below.'

"As I was crossing the field, I heard the first sharp bursts

of machine-gun fire. My heart skipped a beat; this was my
first battle.

"At my post behind the Guillet house, I listened to the
whine of bullets and the roar of the mortars. Unexpectedly,
my father appeared: 'You must go to a higher position. Get
back to the village and stay there until you get new orders.'

"About noon orders came to move down the slope. I
gathered together the stretcher bearers, all quite young fellows, and we piled into an ambulance. There had been heavy
fighting but now all was calm. Probably the Germans were
resting. Some men were waiting for us and I asked them
about my father.

"'He's all right,' they told me. 'The Nazis finally got it
through their thick heads that we mean business. Your father's machine-gun unit was forced to fall back. It reached
its new position just in time to spot some Germans who
were fanning out in a field. The guns got half of them. But
we've had plenty of losses. The Boches have some good
shots on their side. Lieutenant Armand is badly wounded.'

"They escorted us to a grove where our wounded had
been taken. One young man with a jagged wound in his
arm was lying on his back. His dead-white face had a greenish tinge and he kept repeating: 'They got me, the rats.
They got me before I ever had a chance. But I'll pay them
back.'

"Then I saw Lieutenant Armand. He had a gaping wound
in his chest near his heart and blood was streaming down
his legs from ugly wounds in his thighs. He was moaning
softly; when we lifted him onto the stretcher, he cried out,
and when we started to carry him away, he groaned, 'Not
so fast. You're hurting me. Please don't shake me.' Almost
in tears, I tried to make him more comfortable. We walked
as carefully as we could, but still he moaned.

"As the ambulance drove off with the wounded, I went
down to the curve in the rear to watch the fighting, and
two other boys joined me. The Germans renewed their at-

tack on our center and met with stiff resistance. We moved
down toward the houses where we met my father.

" 'What are you doing here?' he asked.

" 'We came to see if we could help,' I told him, 'How's
the fighting going?'

" 'Well, the Nazis are attacking full force, but we drove
them back with grenades. Ittier and his bazooka are working miracles and Roland is handling the mortar himself.'
Then he looked at me sternly. 'But what are you doing here
without orders? Bravery is a fine thing, but there's no sense
in running useless risks.'

" 'Well,' I answered. 'I thought there might be something
I could do, and I was afraid no one would call me because
I'm your son.'

"He laughed and patted me on the shoulder. 'You'll be
called if they need you, never fear. Now go back to your
places.'

"We rejoined our companions. Suddenly the roar of violent explosions was added to the bark of machine guns.
Clouds of black smoke rose in the sky. All of us tore down
to see what was happening.

"When we found my father, he was very happy. 'Did you
see that? A Nazi was blown up right over the trees.'

" 'What happened?' I asked.

" 'Oh, the Germans thought they could take that little hill
by the crossroads. We drove them back with grenades. I
really think the fighting is over for today.'

"We got our stretchers and went out into the field. Now
I came face to face with death for the first time. A man lay
stretched out along an embankment, his machine gun lying
near him." (Perhaps in this instance Michel meant a submachine gun or Sten gun.) "He was dead. At first I was
half afraid to touch him but finally I helped lift him onto
the stretcher. His arm was stiff and sticky with blood and
a great red star was spreading over his face.

"Father took me with him to St. Nizier where the people
gave him a rousing welcome. June 13 was my father's forty-

third birthday and he smiled and said: 'This is a good birthday celebration.'

"That night things had quieted down and he said to me:

"'Look here, son. I've always hoped that some part of France would be able to liberate itself without outside help. Today it seems that my dreams may come true. But you—you must promise me to be more careful in the future.'

"The next day, the Nazis opened a heavy barrage of artillery fire. The following day they launched a mass attack. I spent a lot of time flat on my face. When we had to go out under fire to pick up one of our wounded, I admit I was terrified. The enemy could see us plainly and we couldn't hide because we had to carry the stretcher. But they missed us. As the fighting came closer our men were forced back toward St. Nizier. Four of us had to go out again to bring in another wounded Maquisard but this time I was too excited to be afraid even though bullets whizzed between us. Maybe I was getting used to war.

"Later, I was told that my father had been wounded in the leg but had refused to ride in the commanding officer's car. Instead he had gone back into the hills with his men.

"When we moved into our new position, I went with Dr. Bailly and the first company into the mountains. We had three whole days of rain and then it snowed for three days. We had almost nothing to eat. Then I was granted leave and was able to visit my father at Meaudre. That was a happy time. We talked together of all sorts of things, even of mathematics, music and literature." (In his account Michel does not mention here any wound suffered by his father, indicating that this had either been a false report or that the wound was a negligible one.)

"This respite was short. Beginning July 14, Bastille Day, German planes bombed the Vercors plateau almost daily. On July 21, the enemy sent two divisions to storm the plateau while Nazi paratroopers occupied Vessieux and the landing field."

Although Michel could not possibly realize it, the aerial

assault was the disaster point of the battle. At first cheers had resounded on the plateau when planes were seen approaching. These must be the expected Allied aerial reinforcements! By the time the Maquisards realized they were enemy craft, no kind of effective antiaircraft fire could be organized. Twenty big battle planes towing as many glider planes landed smoothly and disgorged elite paratroopers armed to the teeth. The paratroopers immediately dug in and opened devastating fire in many directions with submachine guns, machine guns, mortars and light artillery. Now the French were under attack from the outside and the inside.

"For three days, 24,000 Maquisards held out against terrific odds," Michel recalled. "Although the Germans did not attack the Jarrands sector where I was stationed, for three days I could hear the big guns pounding Herbonilly, Caraçon, and Val Chevriere.

"My father was holding one of these positions with two companies. The Nazis attacked him with two regiments. On the afternoon of the third day, my father ordered his men to fall back into the Grotte des Fées (Grotto of the Fairies), a sparkling underworld of stalactites and stalagmites.

"Meanwhile, we, too, had been forced back. In the dead of night we climbed down a steep cliff. My feet were cut and bleeding from the jagged rocks; my eyes were riveted on the knapsack of the man in front of me. Clinging to the cliff with my right hand, I felt along the edge of the precipice with my left foot. It was a sickening sensation whenever I encountered yawning space.

"Finally we were down. In small groups we hid in the tangled underbrush of a deep forest. German soldiers were on the lookout for us and patrolled the roads in groups of 60 to 150. Sometimes they even patrolled the woods and often passed very near our hiding places. We went out to get water early in the morning or late at night. The Nazis never dared go abroad in small groups after dark. Several times we were almost discovered. We lived in constant fear of a surprise attack.

"One day the doctor came and took me with him to the Duffaud company, stationed near Autrans. For twenty hours steadily, we climbed thickly wooded slopes and scurried over exposed rocky sectors, until we reached the encampment which was entrenched behind natural barriers of rocks. Staggering from exhaustion I was ready to sleep on my feet, when I saw the commanding officer coming toward me.

"'Michel, have you heard the news?' he said.

"I stared at him blankly saying, 'What news?'

"He spoke to me gently: 'Your father is dead.'

"The mountain peaks seemed to surge upward and crash together. I was so tired it all felt like a nightmare. Commander Durieux put his hand on my shoulder to steady me.

"'Yes, Michel, the Nazis ambushed him on his way to Grenoble. He was killed instantly.'

"I don't remember much of the next few days. Shock and exhaustion had made me ill. The FFI took care of me in a nearby farmhouse and all the time I lay in a fever I said over and over: 'It's not true, it's not true.'

"The Germans were finally withdrawn from Vercors and Dr. Bailly released me to go home. As far as I was concerned, the war was over. I was too young to join the regular armed forces."

There was no quarter in this battle. Not many French escaped. There were no prisoners, no wounded, only dead.

The Germans were not content with battle victory. They were in the grip of half-crazed Teutonic fury and carried out one of those reprisal actions which so often shocked the world during the war.

Town after town in the region was destroyed. At La Chapelle-en-Vercors, where there never had been any fighting, the Germans assembled the entire population in the village square, locked the women and children in the schoolhouse, methodically looted the village and destroyed everything that they did not think worthy of taking away in

trucks. Then they set fire to every building but the schoolhouse, and slaughtered every male inhabitant between the
ages of fourteen and sixty. The rampage lasted nearly
twenty-four hours. Those who survived recalled that the officer commanding was very polite and calm throughout the
operation.

Just what happened to the village of La Mure will never
be fully known. There were no survivors here. Mystery pre-
vails to this day as to the fate of the men of the village,
except for two of them. These two were found hanged
from an ingenious scaffold at the entrance of the village.
The scaffold was so designed that each man had one foot on
the ground. The first one to collapse would cause the rope
to strangle both of them. They had no eyes left, no tongues.
What particularly shocked French investigators who entered
the village shortly after the battle was a small fire-blackened
house near the edge of the village. The women and children
of the village had been locked in this building and roasted
to death. Even the cats and dogs of the village had been
shot.

A woman schoolteacher aged seventy was one of the heroines of these frightful hours. She taught at the township of
Beaufort. The Germans had blown up most of Beaufort
when they advanced on the school, obviously prepared to
do the same to that building. The teacher met them in the
doorway fearlessly and gave them such a tongue-lashing
about their actions that the Germans finally were ashamed
and left without destroying the school or any other buildings.

They might not have left so tamely had they known who
the woman was. The schoolteacher was the secretary of the
local resistance organization. In the basement of the school
was a veritable arsenal of ammunition, rifles, and other
equipment for the Maquis.

There is a brief statement which is a personal epilogue
to this story of the Vercors. It was penned by Michel
Prévost when he told his story after the liberation.

"Today I am just an average French schoolboy, studying hard. I still cannot accept the fact that I, who was in the thick of battle and saw men fight and die, am still considered a mere boy. I was old enough to fight; today I can't even drink coffee after dinner. They give me candy."

COLLISION COURSE

The Germans could achieve victory in massive attacks against a specific objective but there was a battle they never won—the battle of the rails.

Almost to a man, the French railwaymen were resistants in one capacity or another. They had a great tactical advantage—the Germans could not supplant them en masse, they could merely place supervisors over them.

Their sabotage methods ran the gamut from small derailments to real movie spectaculars. The *Apfelkern* incident was just one of many. Trains intended for Germany with supplies of all kinds or other trains scheduled to provide arms for various troop concentrations were skillfully rerouted and wound up at some unscheduled, distant point. Locomotives would start smoothly on a trip and suddenly break down, blocking an entire track. Signals would go wrong and electric current feeding this type of transportation would suddenly go dead for days. Railway workers on many occasions would coordinate attacks on trains by the Maquisards, informing the raiders when a train would reach a favorable attacking point. Frequently railwaymen, once the day's work was over, would slip away and join in such attacks. Also in the ranks of the railwaymen were special agents sent from England, men specifically trained in this type of sabotage, all masquerading as French railwaymen.

For the Germans the entire battle of the rails was a hydra-headed monster in France as well as other occupied countries. The Germans, of course, retaliated swiftly when they had proof that a railwayman had done sabotage. Execution guns crackled.

A striking example of railway sabotage occurred in the vicinity of Besançon, in eastern France, near the Swiss border.

As far as the Germans were concerned the scene of this attack was aptly named. It occurred near an elevation known as the Mountain of Miserey. It was carried out by four young Maquisards at the time of the Allied landings in Normandy.

On a sunny summer day the four, armed and equipped with heavy tools needed for unscrewing rails, left the Maquis camp in a forested area and headed for the Mount Miserey zone. They knew that a rather important supply train on the Vesoul line would pass through that region late in the morning. They unscrewed rails in a gully. The train came thundering along. Rails buckled and the locomotive and most of the cars immediately behind it zoomed off the track and overturned.

Unfortunately, a German truck full of soldiers was passing along at the time and spotted the Maquisards in a nearby hill position. Both the Germans and the Maquisards opened fire. While this engagement was underway one of the Maquisards, named Philippe, slipped away with the full knowledge of his companions and headed for the Miserey railway station. Here he found another train and ordered the railwaymen there to start it at full speed and send it down the track where the wreck was. This was done and that train hurtled into the wreck in the gully with awesome impact. This new incident broke up the armed engagement and the three Maquisards escaped, soon rejoined by Philippe.

The next day Philippe, unarmed and in everyday clothing, bicycled to the area where the trains had been wrecked. By this time the *Gestapo* and soldiers were there, examining tracks and questioning civilians and railwaymen.

Philippe cycled past quietly, inwardly very gleeful, and again headed for the Miserey station. There was a locomotive with steam up on the tracks. The irrepressible Philippe saw another glowing opportunity and immediately contacted

the railwaymen present. After some arguing—the railwaymen were a little reluctant to do anything more—Philippe
convinced them that action was absolutely necessary. As a
result this locomotive, a big one, and its tender and a freight
car, were sent off at full speed in the right direction. Philippe
then bicycled for the hills.

The Maquis band learned later from onlookers that the
locomotive hit the wreckage in the gully while the *Gestapo*
were still there. The locomotive plowed into the overturned
cars and locomotives like a thunderclap. It leaped thirty
feet into the air and landed upside down on some overturned cars, its wheels spinning, enveloped in hissing steam.

The *Gestapo* scurried away in all directions, along with
anyone else in the vicinity when the steel monster swooped
down. The Germans soon returned and continued their investigation. Such an event could not be kept secret. Soon
crowds of curious were in the vicinity.

Philippe was not through. On the following day, enroute
to Besançon on his bicycle accompanied by another Maquisard, he spotted another train which he routed where it
would do the most harm. It added stature to the wreckage.

For days crowds of curious cycled or walked to the area
to see for themselves what had occurred. The pile-up was
locally referred to as the mountain of Miserey. To all
Gestapo questioning railwaymen replied that this was the
work of Maquisards who had threatened them with death
unless their orders were heeded. The railway workers furnished so many alibis that none of them could be convicted.
The Vesoul line was out of commission for weeks.

Jestkrieg

In the midst of all the terror and danger of the secret war,
the people of France and other countries evolved their own
jestkrieg to offset Hitler's blitzkrieg. It was great fun for
everyone except the Germans.

A few days after the Nazis entered Paris in 1940, an old
lady of seventy-eight helped momentarily to dispel the

depression of many inhabitants of the city. She was one of the first resistants and went underground in the full sense of the word.

This Frenchwoman spent many happy hours sitting on a small stool in one of the capital's busiest subway stations. She had a long cane in one hand. The cane snaked out when any German passed close enough to be within reach. She aimed for the booted area between the knees and ankles. A quick twist of the cane and the victim would stumble or take a full fall.

The Germans thus attacked could do nothing more than curse the old lady who seemingly did not see too well and mumbled double-talk which could be taken for apology. Her score on good days sometimes was as high as thirty or forty Germans, officers and men in the ranks. She kept this up for weeks but when fall came she suspended operations due to the cold. Her name is not known but her *beau geste* is remembered by many Parisians who saw her in action.

The French resistance will always be a milestone in man's struggle to achieve a better world in which tyranny and the belief that super people exist have no place. It was largely a battle of the young—four-fifths of the resistants being under thirty.

The price was heavy. Thirty thousand shot, 115,000 deported. Of the latter only 40,000 returned to France.

3

Denmark

"Be hard . . . Be without mercy.
The citizens of Western Europe must
quiver in horror. . . ."

*Adolf Hitler in a statement to
German military commanders on
August 22, 1939*

CANARY INTO DRAGON

The events which occurred in Hans Christian Andersen land after April 9, 1940—when the Hitlerian colossus struck northward in Europe—had overtones evoking tales by the fabulous storyteller of Odense himself.

In the fair land there was a good king, his queen, and their loyal countrymen, the bullying henchmen of an infamous tyrant, and a mythical canary: a canary which grew into a dragon with fangs and talons, hydra-headed, visible yet invisible, which dueled by day and by night with the Hitlerian foe.

The dragon was the Danish anti-Nazi resistance.

Sovereign of this small country was lean, tall, and gentlemanly King Christian X. He could be seen almost every day riding a handsome horse through the streets of Copenhagen where the famous harbor landmark, the carved likeness of Andersen's Little Mermaid, stares wistfully seaward. No bodyguards followed the knightly monarch around. His guardians were the people themselves. The King and members of his family were beloved by all Danes except for a handful of rogues who thought that Hitler was a jolly good fellow.

The land where Prince Hamlet brooded in Elsinore's Kronborg Castle, where Andersen penned stories which would delight young and old, had known peace for decades. It had last known invasion in 1864, a brief struggle with Bismarck's rampaging Prussians in which Denmark was downed and had to cede considerable territory.

On April 9, 1940, Denmark's happy state came to an end.

On that fateful day all citizens of Copenhagen and vicinity were awakened by an unknown terrifying noise. They jumped out of bed and ran to the windows. The dawn was still half dusky and more so because the sky was blackened by enormous and slow-roaring bombers. They flew so low that many people had the feeling that they could not avoid tearing the rooftops off the houses.

"If the ground under them had opened up and an earthquake had swallowed the houses, the Danes could not have been more awe-struck. They did not scream, they did not even cry; their faces whitened, they felt cold as if touched by death itself. They were told nothing in those early hours but after the first shock they understood." *

Hitler was striking not only against Denmark but at Norway as well, where a brother of King Christian, Haakon VII, was on the throne.

In less than twenty-four hours the Germans swarmed in by land, sea, and air—suddenly, treacherously—making the two countries the first targets of Hitler's armed eruption in the west. As usual, Hitler proclaimed he was a friendly champion hurrying northward to thwart sinister designs against both countries by his archenemy, Britain, but this was so much lamb's wool speckling a wolf's body.

He calmly trampled on an official document which should have proven a shield to King Christian's land. On May 31, 1939, Denmark, alone among the northern nations, had signed a non-aggression pact offered by Hitler's government. It was supposed to be valid for ten years.

The dual swoop, which tossed all concepts of chivalrous warfare into the ashcan, wrote finis to the so-called phony

---

* Karin Michaelis in the chapter devoted to Denmark in the book *The Sixth Column.*

war in western Europe. There were no formal declarations of war, just ultimatums presented by German diplomatic envoys in Copenhagen and Oslo containing clear-cut warnings that any resistance to German occupation would have dire consequences.

When the demands were presented early on April 9, the German operations already were underway, meticulously planned in previous months. German military commanders were in Copenhagen, the Danish capital, and Norway's capital, Oslo, posing as civilians. Danish and Norwegian pro-Nazis had been alerted, all of them ready to cooperate. Ships masquerading as peaceful merchantmen were either enroute to the two countries or already in Norwegian and Danish harbors, ready to disgorge German combat troops hidden in their holds. German warships were closing in by sea and swarms of Luftwaffe planes headed for vital points near and far from Reich bases.

Of the two operations, the Norwegian take-over was the most important event in view of this country's greater size, its terrain far more defensible than that of Denmark, and its over-all strategic significance. Nonetheless, little Denmark in the long run would play just as vital a part as its larger neighbor in the secret war against the Nazis.

The seizure of Denmark was easy for the Germans. Its armed forces consisted of some 15,000 men plus a small fleet and a negligible air force.

Some scattered fighting did occur involving less than a hundred casualties, both Danish and German. The odds were hopeless, the whole onslaught too rapid for any organized armed defense. Before day's end King Christian and his government sorrowfully consented to German occupation to spare the country the horrors of war, such as had befallen Poland. The King decided not to flee from the country. He maintained this decision and would prove an inspiration to his subjects throughout the long and difficult years ahead.

The Germans lulled the Danes with sweeping promises

that they would not meddle with internal affairs, including such divisions as the press, police, the army and navy, that the only change would be the presence of German forces in the country acting in a protective capacity. These promises would not stand up for very long, the velvet glove a transient mirage.

Hitler had some bright hopes regarding the country. He planned to transform it into a model protectorate which would prove to the whole world how beneficial a friendly German occupation could be.

In the beginning the Germans were very punctilious, very courteous, all friendliness. Resistance of various kinds, notably distribution of illegal newspapers and pamphlets and the cold shoulder treatment for the Germans did flare up almost immediately. However, resistance did not become widespread as soon as in other countries due to the fact that the Germans initially avoided doing anything which would arouse the Danes to fighting pitch.

While Hitler had his own idea regarding Denmark, Winston Churchill, then British First Lord of the Admiralty, had his own and lost little time in stating it in a pithy declaration. He said bluntly that the "sadistic murderer" (Hitler) intended to make Denmark his canary. What no one could foresee at that time was that the canary was destined to grow into a very rambunctious and dangerous bird. By the time the Danes were through with their protector, their underground exploits would be hailed as second to none by British Field Marshal Bernard Montgomery and other Allied leaders.

The honor of being the first persons to distribute illegal anti-Nazi literature in a western European occupied land probably belongs to a handful of Copenhagen teen-age students. The action was modest but extremely prompt. Some four hours after the first Germans entered Copenhagen, seventeen-year-old Arne Sejr and some of his student friends were on the city's streets. Darting from person to person or groups of persons, they distributed some twenty-

odd copies of a mimeographed leaflet they had composed.
It urged, in part:

You must work badly for the Germans.
You must work slowly for the Germans.
You must spoil whatever helps the Germans.
You must defend every person persecuted by the Germans.
JOIN THE FIGHT FOR DENMARK'S FREEDOM!

There were several thousand Danes who were able to
undertake immediate and effective resistance. These were
Danish seamen whose crafts were in various waters on
April 9 beyond Hitler's reach. They immediately headed
for Allied ports. Their many ships proved a vital aid to the
Allies in the war, their crews writing heroic pages in the
annals of the sea.

Not all Danish territory was occupied on April 9. The
Faroe Islands and Greenland were outside German reach.
Through the action of Danish diplomatic envoys abroad,
British troops were stationed in the Faroes. The Danish
Minister to the United States, Henrik de Kauffman, signed
an agreement with Washington whereby American bases
could be established in Greenland. A Danish sledge patrol
thwarted German plans to establish meteorological stations
in this great Arctic territory, involving the Danes in direct
military operations against the Germans.

"Submission on April 9th was only the beginning of the
concessions made to the Germans by the Danish Government," Jorgen Haestrup, noted historian of the Danish resistance, stated in a Danish official publication.

"During the years 1940-43 the government constantly
gave way to renewed German demands," he added. "The
Germans plundered the country, applied censorship, inter-
fered with the administration of justice, demanded the surrender of Danish warships, required her participation in the
Anti-Comintern pact (aimed against Communism) and made
other demands.

"The resistance movement developed as a protest against

this policy of conciliation . . . at home there were increasing demands, especially among the youth of the country, that Denmark should enter into direct conflict against the Nazis. . . .

"In 1943 it became obvious that the nation no longer supported the policy of conciliation. A great wave of sabotage swept over the country, accompanied by widespread strikes. The Germans made new demands on the government, among other things insisting on the introduction to the death penalty. The government's answer to this was in the negative and on August 29, 1943, the Germans attacked the Danish Army and fleet. The government ceased to function and the Germans openly took over power in the country."

Denmark had been allowed to retain a small army and the control of her navy. In a few hours the Danish military was rounded up and generally neutralized. Its officers and men were interned, with the exception of those who were able to go underground and join the resistance forces. The Danish armed forces, however, did succeed in striking a solid blow. Before the Germans pounced, some twenty-nine ships of Denmark's navy had been scuttled and many others so badly damaged by their crews that they were beyond repair. Thirteen ships escaped to Sweden and only thirteen small vessels fell into German hands. The Danish government resigned and the King became a prisoner in his own land.

THE DANISH PIMPERNELS

Hitler's attempt to make Denmark *Judenrein* (cleansed of Jews) ended in a Night and Fog of its own with the Nazis gnashing their teeth.

Up to the fall of 1943 the Germans had maintained a hands-off policy toward Denmark's Jews, approximately 8000 of them, 95 per cent of them residing in Copenhagen and its environs. This was due in large part to the fact that Hitler's top man in Denmark, Dr. Werner Best, was convinced that any drastic action against the Jews would have explosive results in that country. He was right. But Hitler, obsessed with his plans for a final solution of the Jewish problem, could not be deflected from his purpose, in spite of the small number of Jews involved.

Imperative orders came from Berlin. The Nazis evolved secret plans to seize virtually all the Danish Jews in one big swipe that fall. It was timed for the day of Rosh Hashana, the Jewish New Year, which fell on October 1. Some seven thousand Jews simply vanished right under the Nazi noses.

Strangely enough, in this case one of the persons who threw a monkey wrench in Hitler's plans was a German by the name of Georg Ferdinand Duckwitz. In view of what happened his name was rather apt, since "to duck" means a manner of escaping a blow and "witz" means a joke in German.

Duckwitz had come to Denmark in 1928 after graduation from law school and had taken a position in a German coffee concern in Copenhagen. After the occupation he had been given a post in the German embassy as head of shipping in Copenhagen. Fortunately for the Jews, Duckwitz was no rabid Nazi and did not approve of Hitler's anti-Semitic policies. During their stay in Denmark Duckwitz and his wife had made many friends among the Danes, including the leaders of the important Danish Social Democrat Party.

The official's first inkling of German plans to arrest Danish Jews came on September 11, 1943, when Nazi plenipotentiary Best informed him of pressure being put on him by Hitler himself to crack down on Jews in Denmark. Duckwitz made it plain to Best that he personally would be ashamed to participate in any such persecution.

Now Duckwitz became something of an underground operator himself. He flew to Berlin on September 13. Information he obtained there proved that Hitler was determined to launch a major, secret action in Denmark against the Jews. Returning to Copenhagen, Duckwitz learned that

Germans in civilian clothes had broken into the Jewish Community Center offices and had stolen records containing the names and addresses of Jewish members.

In view of Duckwitz' position in the embassy, Best on the following day informed him that on September 29 German ships would anchor in Copenhagen harbor ready to take on thousands of Jews, their ultimate destination Theresienstadt concentration camp. The Jews would be arrested in lightning raids, he learned.

Courageously, knowing fully what risks he ran, Duckwitz decided to act fast on behalf of the Jews. On his own initiative he flew to Stockholm on September 25 and conferred with Swedish Prime Minister Per Albin Hansson. He convinced the Swedish government that it was imperative it notify Berlin that Sweden would be ready to receive all of Denmark's Jews as refugees. Stockholm sent a telegram to this effect. Duckwitz flew back to Copenhagen after being informed that the Swedish embassy there would notify him of Berlin's reply.

Two days passed and no news from the Swedish embassy. On Thursday evening, September 29, Duckwitz rightly assumed that the Germans had spiked the Stockholm telegram. Unquestionably the raid would take place and the Jews would be caught virtually en masse in the Copenhagen area while observing Rosh Hashana in their homes and synagogues.

That evening the German made up his mind that he must give warning to the Danes. Duckwitz rushed to 22 Roemer Street in Copenhagen where he knew that the Social Democrats were having a meeting.

"White with indignation and shame" Duckwitz entered the main meeting room and walked swiftly up to Hans Hedtoft, head of the Social Democratic party.

"The disaster is here," he told him, his voice trembling. "Everything is planned in detail. In a few hours ships will anchor in the harbor of Copenhagen. Those of your poor Jewish countrymen who get caught will forcibly be brought

on board the ships and transported to an unknown fate."
Then he left as hurriedly as he had come, knowing his
life was in grave danger. Convinced he was telling the truth,
Hedtoft personally notified C. B. Henriques, head of the
Jewish Community, of the danger. Somewhat to his dismay,
Henriques refused to believe the information, lulled by as-
surances from a Danish government official that he had
been informed by Best that nothing would happen.

Returning to the meeting place, the downcast Hedtoft
informed his friends of Henriques' attitude. They decided,
however, that they must spread the warning.

By telephone and personal visits they conveyed the tidings
to Jewish and non-Jewish people. The news spread quickly,
secretly in Copenhagen and elsewhere. Many who had
never participated in any serious form of resistance went
into action.

Danish "Pimpernels" were scurrying everywhere and plans
were being formulated to hide as many Jews as possible and
somehow get them to Sweden and safety.

Typical of the impromptu methods evolved by the Danes
was the case of Jorgen Knudsen, a young ambulance driver.
He was leaving his apartment to report for work when he
noticed some students who were friends of his rushing up
and down the street stopping people. When they informed
him of the news, he stormed, "So the bastards have finally
decided to do this. Damn them all!"

Knudsen, like virtually all Danes, had never thought in
terms of Jewish or non-Jewish friends. Religious factors did
not enter into his conception of friendship. He wanted to
do something quickly to help but could not think at the
moment of a single friend with a Jewish-sounding name.
A telephone booth nearby gave him an inspiration. He
entered it and ripped out the telephone directory. Hiding it
under his coat, he walked rapidly to the garage where his
ambulance was parked. In the garage he opened the directory
and checked off with a pencil all those names which sounded
Jewish to him. He did not report for work at the big

While the Germans built almost impregnable gun fortifications to guard the French coast against Allied invasion, the French underground reported their locations to Allied force headquarters in England. *(French Embassy Press & Information Division)*

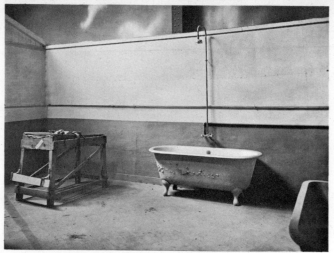

Underground activity had many hazards, the greatest of which was capture for interrogation by the brutal *Gestapo*. Photos show torture instruments routinely used by the German Secret State Police in their savage questionings to obtain information from the underground fighters. Photo shows a torture room. Close-up below shows pincers for pulling off fingernails, club for beating the soles of the feet, and manacles for holding prisoner during interrogation. *(French Embassy Press & Information Division)*

This French resistant shows defiance of the Nazi tyrants by smiling as the German non-commissioned officer in charge calls the last
sounds the underground fighter will ever hear: Ready! Aim! Fire!
(French Embassy Press & Information Division)

The blind Jacques Lussey-
ran, shown here in a recent
photograph, was a teen-age
leader of a vast network of
young French underground
operators. He now lives in
Cleveland, Ohio, and teaches
at Western Reserve University. *(Jack Palmer, courtesy
Little, Brown and Company)*

3

Jean Prevost, whose story is told in the words of his son in *Gallic Thermopylae*, was a Maquis officer killed in the great fight at the *Vercors* near Grenoble in the French Alps where the French resistance fighters faced the Germans in pitched battle. *(French Embassy Press & Information Division)*

Even the teen-agers of France joined the Maquis and took up arms against the German conquerors. This boy was a member of a group that harassed German communications and transportation. He may now be living in France or he may have died in the service of his country. *(French Embassy Press & Information Division)*

Joseph Parrachine was a soldier at age thirteen. At the time this picture was taken, he and his unit had been in several hit-and-run battles against German troops and tanks. *(French Embassy Press & Information Division)*

4

The Maquis were an irregular army headquartered here and there in secrecy, dressed in whatever clothes they took from home, and armed with captured weapons. Here a group of Maquisards are receiving training in the use of the famous Sten gun, held in the hands of the man at left. *(French Embassy Press & Information Division)*

In France, people from all walks of life responded to the call of freedom. Here a French priest directs fighters in the battle of Paris. *(French Embassy Press & Information Division)*

The Germans occupied Norway early in the war, still the Norwegians were never defeated. Max Manus, left, and Gregers Gram, right, were typical fighters in the Norwegian underground armies. Their specialty was sabotaging German vessels in Norwegian harbors. Gregers Gram was trapped and shot by Germans posing as Norwegian sympathizers. Max Manus still lives in Norway.

One of the greatest underground victories was the sabotage and destruction of the airdrome in Aalborg, Denmark. Anton Toldstrup, shown here in a photograph taken just after the final German defeat, was one of the underground strategists who planned this blow that severely damaged the German war effort. (*Kai Winkelhorn*)

Danish resistance secret headquarters. Threatened by German raids, resistants could enter the cupboard, close the door behind them, and vanish into a garden via the secret passage.

Girls, too, were active in the underground. This Norwegian girl, shown in a photograph taken during the occupation, is typing the latest news from the war fronts for use in underground newspapers. The pistol on the box was probably meant for suicide in case of capture rather than defense. *(Norsk Telegrambyras)*

The railroads, so necessary in moving troops, were a particular target of the undergrounds everywhere. This locomotive was derailed in France in July of 1944. *(French Embassy Press & Information Division)*

Bispebjerg Hospital that day. Instead he drove throughout
Copenhagen calling on total strangers to give them the warning. When Jews he contacted became alarmed because they
had no one to turn to to go into hiding, Knudsen piled
them into his ambulance. Then he drove them to the
hospital where he knew that the hospital chief, Dr. Karl
Henry Koster, would be willing to hide them.

One of the first to be notified was Rabbi Marcus Melchior of the Copenhagen Synagogue, a venerable structure
built more than a century ago. On Friday morning, September 30, 1943, he stood before the Holy Ark and solemnly
addressed 150 members of the congregation, all of them puzzled by the fact that he was not wearing rabbinical robes.

"There will be no service this morning," he said.

After informing them that the Germans planned to raid
Jewish homes, he added: "We must take action immediately.
You must leave the synagogue now and contact all relatives,
friends, and neighbors you know are Jewish and tell them
what I have told you. You must tell them to pass the word
on to everyone they know is Jewish. You must also speak
to all your Christian friends and tell them to warn the Jews.
You must do this immediately, within the next few minutes,
so that two or three hours from now everyone will know
what is happening: by nightfall tonight we must all be in
hiding."

Melchior, his wife, and five children hurriedly left Copenhagen and hid with a friend, Pastor Hans Kildeby, Lutheran
minister at Orslev, sixty miles south of Copenhagen. As if
by magic thousands of Jews were secreted in homes, apartments, business offices, lofts, hospitals, farmhouses, cellars,
and churches, and cared for by untold numbers of Danes.
A small number refused to heed the warning for various
reasons and did not go into hiding.

A few days previous Best had ignored a letter from King
Christian advising him that any action against the Jews
would have "most severe consequences" in Denmark where

for more than a hundred years they had enjoyed full citizenship rights.

Shortly before midnight, September 29, two German transport vessels dropped anchor in Copenhagen harbor. Late on the following day the Germans went into action with a bang. Wehrmacht companies cordoned off the harbor area. *Gestapo* and special commandos raced like bloodhounds through the streets. Another Tag was at hand—virtually all of Denmark's Jews would be in the bag in short order, the Germans believed. Brimmingly confident, Herr Best sent a premature victory telegram to his big boss in Berlin:

"It was my duty to clean Denmark of her Jews and this is achieved. Denmark is judenrein and is completely purged."

Throughout that weekend the Germans, getting more frantic hourly, armed with address lists, raided the residences of Danish Jews, virtually all of them located in Copenhagen or its environs.

The trophies of this mass hunt were fantastically low in number. With the exception of some two hundred Jews who had not heeded the warning—generally because they were too old or too ill to go into hiding—they had evaporated into thin air. No one was "at home." It was clear that something had gone very much amiss for the Germans.

When news of the failure reached Berlin, Hitler and Himmler, according to eyewitness accounts, became "raging mad with indignation."

Hurriedly Adolf dispatched his arch Jew-killer, Adolf Eichmann, to Copenhagen. He arrived there on October 3 and verbally tore into Best and any other official involved in the operation. It did no good.

The big ship *Wartheland*, outfitted to hold thousands of prisoners, weighed anchor and headed for Germany. There was plenty of room for the prisoners aboard—if that could be termed any consolation. The Jewish prisoners still numbered 202. The other transport also weighed anchor for the Reich. There were no Jews at all on this ship.

In a few days Eichmann left Denmark for more urgent killing business in eastern Europe. Before departing he gave strict orders that the raids were to continue, that the Jews were to be found at all costs. It was impossible, he believed, for the Danish Jews to remain in hiding for more than a few days.

The Danes, of course, also realized that it was imperative to get the Jews to Sweden as soon as possible by any kind of water transportation available. With the aid of various resistance groups, now united under the aegis of the Danish Freedom Council, Danes in all walks of life plunged into the task. Owners of boats, mostly fishing craft, were contacted and pledged themselves to aid in the evacuation. Funds were donated by non-Jewish and Jewish Danes to pay for transportation since the boatowners asked payment for passengers whose presence on board ship would constitute a constant danger. To the credit of most of the seamen they usually did not ask too exorbitant fares, generally some $60 per person, and often took Jews across for nothing.

Doctors and nurses played stellar roles in smuggling Jews out. Huge numbers were sheltered in such medical institutions as the Bispebjerg Hospital and the Rockefeller Institute in Copenhagen, listed as patients, registered under assumed names until such a time as they could be routed to the coast. At various times nurses' quarters were packed with scores of Jewish men, women, and children. Every bit of food that could be spared was funneled to the hidden Jews, both in hospitals and elsewhere. Amid the daily tensions and fears, there were some unusual incidents.

One young Jewish man in a hospital was given so many useless stomach pumpings to keep up the illusion he was sick in case any informers were around that he finally told the doctors that they might as well turn him over to the *Gestapo* since he could not stand such attention any more. He was soon convinced that no such thing must happen and eventually reached Sweden in excellent health.

On several occasions very young Jewish children in hiding or awaiting transportation to the boats were given sedative injections by doctors so that their noisemaking would not betray them to the Germans. The threat of a German "Halt!" and search was ever-present both on land and sea. A hospital truck driver transporting a number of escapees was stopped by a German patrol in the Copenhagen area. Hearing some mumbled exclamations in the back of the truck, a German soldier sharply asked the driver who the other passengers were. The driver thought quickly and replied "Oh, those are some lunatics we are transferring to a hospital for the insane." This was enough for the German and the truck was permitted to pass.

The Germans had tightened measures to prevent flight by sea. Virtually every type of small boat had been ordered transported inland for some 1000 yards, fishing boats excepted. As a result the sea transportation depended almost exclusively on fishermen. Some boats were intercepted and some Jews were captured but their number was amazingly small.

THE CHURCHILL CLUB AND OTHER EPISODES

The Nazi hunters were run ragged by some very tricky "game" in the Danish city of Aalborg in north Jutland. This was the Churchill Club, all of its members teen-agers endowed with exceptional daring and ingenuity.

Adopting the British Royal Air Force blue, red, and white insignia as their club emblem, these boys secured arms and explosives by theft or other means and proceeded to sabotage German-controlled rail, shipping, and telegraphic communications with considerable success. These will-o'-the-wisps unfailingly left pieces of circular cardboard bearing the RAF colors on the scenes of their exploits, which occurred in the early phase of the occupation.

Finally three of the ringleaders were caught as they prepared to drop hand grenades on Germans from the high
tower of the city's ancient Saint Budolfi Cathedral. Fortunately, the Germans were obliged under existing conditions
to turn them over to Danish authorities for punishment.
They were sentenced to a prison term by a friendly judge
to keep them out of *Gestapo* hands and incarcerated in a
Danish-controlled jail. This was not the end of the road
for the trio by any means.

They persuaded a jailer to permit one of their club pals to
bring various types of material and tools to the cell—so
that they could build model airplanes! The material delivered
soon included a couple of files. While pretending to be busy
for hours making model airplanes, the trio sawed at the bars
of their prison window. This was done in such a manner
that the bars could be separated so as to permit the passage
of a human body and then put back in place.

At night the three crawled through the window, dropped
to a wall below and from there into the street. Mysterious
attacks were renewed in the city, including the cutting of
an important telephone cable and a train derailment. In each
instance the cardboard insignia were found in the vicinity
of the area where the operations occurred. Everything
pointed to the three but angry German policemen could
witness for themselves that the ringleaders were in prison
busy with model airplane problems.

The trio might have been able to keep this up for the
duration of their sentence but for a piece of bad luck.
While they were in action one night a British air attack
occurred in the Aalborg area. In seeking shelter they were
caught by a German patrol, suspicious of their presence in
the streets at such a time. The ringleaders were again im-
prisoned by Danish authorities acting under German pressure. This time they were given no opportunity to work
their way out at night. This brought an end to the club's
operations.

During the occupation the people of Denmark had their moments of laughter or chuckling, either as the result of anti-Nazi jokes or various types of wartime episodes.

On one occasion British fliers bombed and hit a munitions factory built by the Germans in northern Jutland. The Germans, anxious as usual to minimize damage caused by Allied fliers, outdid themselves on this occasion. Since at the time they controlled the press, all papers had to print an announcement that only a cow had been hit in a field and had burned to death.

A local paper, published in a town close to the scene of the bombing, chose to embellish the announcement with one line: "And the cow burned for four days."

As was expected, the newspaper was suspended for two weeks by the Germans and the editor was forced to resign.

During the 1940 period when the Germans were predicting finis for England, a newsdealer in occupied Copenhagen prominently displayed a textbook entitled *English in 50 hours*. Behind the book was a big poster on which he had written LEARN ENGLISH BEFORE THE TOMMIES ARRIVE!

Angered Germans forced him to remove the whole display. The next day the Dane had something new. A textbook entitled *German in 50 hours*, complemented by an even larger placard stating LEARN GERMAN BEFORE OUR FRIENDS, THE GERMANS, LEAVE US!

King Christian himself had top billing in a whole series of anecdotes, some of which were harmlessly fanciful, others based on fact.

According to one tale the King, on his daily ride through Copenhagen, observed a Nazi flag flying on top of a public building. He protested to the German officer in charge on the grounds that this was a violation of Danish-German occupation agreements.

"Orders from Berlin, your Majesty!" the officer replied somewhat arrogantly.

"The flag must be removed before noon. Otherwise I

shall send a Danish soldier to take it down!" the King replied cuttingly.

"The soldier will be shot!" the officer said.

"I am the soldier," the King said and rode away.

OY-DOK

The British-made De Havilland Hornet-Moth biplane, its single Gypsy motor droning, taxied bumpily across the turnip field and into the barley beyond shortly before midnight in the lingering daylight of a Danish summer night.

The man in the bulky civilian clothes running ahead of the light two-seater craft guided it to a point near the edge of the barley field. Then he doubled back and scrambled into the machine.

"Hold tight, Keld, here goes," the man at the controls muttered and gave the ship the gun.

The plane—resembling some aircraft of long ago—wobbled aloft and after banking, headed westward into the night. On its fuselage, printed in big letters, was the word OY-DOK. The letters OY were the Danish civilian craft identification, the others part of this craft's own registration. On this night the plane left the Odense area on the island of Fyn—birthplace of Hans Christian Andersen—forever.

The two men in the plane were young Danes named Thomas C. Sneum and Keld Petersen, both Royal Danish Air Force fliers. Even in normal times the flight would have been very risky. On this night it bordered on the suicidal. A long voyage lay ahead. The plane was in bad shape and the times were not normal. It was June 21, 1941. German troops were within hailing distance of the craft. Aboard the rickety machine was material which, if seized by the Germans, would immediately brand the two fliers as spies.

Second Lieutenant Sneum was in his early twenties when World War II broke out in 1939. He was a blond, blue-eyed flier of medium, athletic build, a hard worker who also

welcomed convivial merriment, good food, and dates with pretty girls.

Stationed at a South Sealand base, he had suspected that Hitler would stomp into Denmark weeks before he did so. When it occurred Sneum, like virtually all Danes, was furious. Some three weeks prior to the take-over Sneum had approached nine of his fellow officers and urged them to fly with him in whatever planes were available to neutral Sweden. The fliers were preparing to do this when their commanding officer got wind of the affair and forbade any such action on the grounds it would constitute desertion.

Before anything further could be organized, the Germans had come. Almost immediately after the occupation, General Ernst Kaupisch, supreme German military commander in Denmark, issued a proclamation which Sneum and many of his fellow officers decided to flout.

"The Danish army and navy will show a spirit of understanding . . ." Kaupisch stated. "By desisting from any passive resistance . . . Such resistance would be unavailing and broken by all forcible means. . . ."

Sneum and other officers, who all belonged to the Royal Danish Fleet Air Arm fighter squadrons, promptly deserted their station, doffed their uniforms for civilian clothes, and more or less went into hiding.

On his own initiative, Sneum began collecting information about German military positions in Denmark. In May 1940 he obtained important information on German plane-detection installations on the west coast island of Fano.

The twenty-six-year-old Dane was eager to convey this and other information he had obtained about the Germans to London. He located a boat in Jutland that would transport him and some of his friends to England. But by the time they were ready to depart, winter ice and storms made the trip unfeasible. Deciding that it would be best for him to remain in Denmark for the time being, Sneum gave whatever information he had to another Danish flying officer,

Kai Oxlund, who was escaping to Sweden, a trip which he completed successfully.

In February 1941 Sneum, bundled up in heavy winter clothing, proceeded to a lonely spot on the Danish coast north of Copenhagen and was rowed across the narrow strip of water dividing Denmark from Sweden by a loyal fisherman. Reaching Stockholm he contacted British officials and gave them new information about German military dispositions in Denmark. He stayed several weeks in the city, proposing to the British to land a Sunderland flying boat on a lake in Denmark. Aboard this craft he and some twenty other Danish officers would be flown to England to join Allied combat groups.

The British agreed to this plan and Sneum returned to Denmark by fishing boat to pursue his intelligence activities. He proceeded to Fano where, equipped with a small motion picture camera, he secretly took pictures of the German installations. He did not know it at the time but he was photographing a Nazi radar complex.

When he was informed that it would be impossible for the British to send the flying boat to the lake, Sneum and several of his friends made plans to escape to England in a small, motor-driven craft which a patriotic fisherman had agreed to relinquish. This plan also had to be scrapped because of sudden increased German coastal vigilance. Realizing that such an attempt was almost certainly doomed, some of the officers fled to Sweden and others dispersed to various parts of Denmark, to bide their time.

Sneum, realizing that if he went again to Sweden he might be interned for the duration, was unflinching in his plan to get to England somehow, and soon. Among the officers was twenty-four-year-old Lieutenant Keld Petersen, a tall, wiry Dane with blond wavy hair. Sneum convinced him that together they could find a way to get to England directly from Denmark. Until then no Dane had succeeded in doing this.

Both returned to Copenhagen after deciding that their

first move would be to obtain a plane in some fashion or other, steal it if necessary. Any airworthy Danish plane had either been impounded by the Germans or was under guard. Sneum then lit on the idea of seeking to secure some civilian craft which was in a state of disrepair and not under close supervision.

Scanning the files of the Danish Civil Aviation Ministry in Copenhagen, Sneum found records of about twenty-five privately owned aircraft in Denmark. He noted that a man named Poul Andersen, owner of a farm named Elsesminde, near the town of Odense, did own a light plane.

Late in April of 1941, two men bicycled up to the main building of the farm and knocked on the door. When Andersen opened it, the shorter of the two men, both of whom were in civilian clothes, said:

"Mr. Andersen, my name is Hansen. I am a civil engineer from Copenhagen, and this is my assistant, Mr. Jensen. I understand you have an airplane on the grounds. Is it possibly for sale?"

"Yes, I do have a plane in that shed you see over there but it is in a pretty sorry state and is not for sale," Andersen replied. "It is a small British-made craft. I was a flier at one time and purchased it some years ago. At one time it was used by the government to carry supplies to icebound people on islands in the Kattegat. The Germans told me I could keep it if I dismantled it. This I did.

"Aside from all this, I really do not want to sell it. Anyhow, you can realize it is all a very poor proposition. It's quite an old bird and lots of work has to be done to put it into any shape whatsoever. The Germans would not let you fly it even if it could be put together again. I will have to say good-day to you."

As Andersen proceeded to close the door his interrogator delayed his action with a hand gesture and said, blue eyes twinkling:

"Now, now, one moment, Mr. Andersen, you mean to

say you would not even sell it if you knew it was headed for England?"

Andersen raised his eyebrows and his lined, sunburned face broke into a smile.

"Ah, that is something else. Come in, come in," he replied.

Convinced that Poul was a loyal Dane and no pro-Nazi the two men immediately informed him that they were Lieutenants Sneum and Petersen of the Danish Fleet Air Arm.

"I will help you in every way I can," Andersen said. "I don't want to sell you the machine but it is at your disposal. It will be very dangerous—a few days ago German troops were stationed in some buildings within shouting distance of this house. You will have to remain in hiding as much as possible in one of my barns. I will give you some old farm clothes to wear. If the Germans should spot you and question you, say you are farm hands I had to hire for spring work. This, we hope, will make sense since I can prove I need help."

The two bikes were then taken to a small, nearby barn and hidden under some canvas in a dark corner. The bundles of clothing strapped to the rear of the bikes were removed and placed in the loft above, where the fliers would sleep. The bundles contained Petersen's and Sneum's air force uniforms, the film of the Fano installations and notes on other German military preparations sewn into their linings.

These were carefully hidden under straw, along with a heavy loaded revolver carried by Petersen. The fliers then donned old shirts and sweaters provided by Andersen.

At dusk the fliers, guided by Andersen, moved silently and cautiously toward the corrugated shed housing the plane, which was on the edge of a turnip field. Borne on the evening breeze, they could hear the voices of German soldiers talking or guffawing beyond a fringe of trees a short distance away.

Even in the dim light Sneum and Petersen could tell that

putting the dismantled biplane together again, not to mention flying it, would be difficult.

Even at that time, in prime condition such a plane already was something of an old-fashioned crate, reminiscent of airplanes of World War I, with many struts and wires, its skeleton fabric-covered, the landing gear non-retractable. Under most favorable weather conditions its top speed was a hundred miles an hour.

Sneum and Petersen looked at the craft with some dismay. The dismantled wings were torn or damaged in various areas. The bolts that had held them in place had been lost and the rubber rudder pedals were gone. The tail fin had been smashed and would have to be rebuilt. A cursory check-up indicated that the engine was fortunately in fairly good condition. Andersen stressed, however, that it would be extremely hazardous to give it any kind of a testing warm-up before the actual take-off because of the vicinity of German troops and the possibility that some Danish turncoat might be within earshot at the time.

On the following day, after a late dinner Sneum and Petersen stealthily entered the shed. All windows were shut and covered with sacking and old newspapers. Andersen had provided various types of tools, several flashlights and candles. The farmer, it had been agreed, would visit the shed as little as possible but would remain on the alert, when not forced to sleep, to warn of any suspicious arrivals or other developments.

That night the two fliers labored on what repairs they could execute, and left at dawn, as secretly as they had come. This activity was repeated during the following evenings. But soon both men realized that the aid of a skilled aviation mechanic would be needed for final assembly. Sneum phoned a mechanic he knew in Copenhagen who joined them, ostensibly a farm hand hired for temporary work.

The three men debated at some length on whether or not all insignia should be removed or painted over. Large Danish flags had been painted on the silver fuselage, near the identification letters OY-DOK. The men finally decided not to paint over the insignia—a conclusion which eventually proved very wise.

Carefully setting the wings in place, they tightened bolts that had been made secretly in an Odense factory atop the worn, dark-gray circles of the original bolts' washers. There was no way to tell if the crisscrossed wires between the wings were drawn to the correct tension. Sneum decided not to bother to improvise rudder pedals because the Moth would have to make just one landing.

Sometimes the men heard German voices in or outside their nearby quarters. On several occasions German soldiers, returning from a spree in Odense, passed so close that their raucous, drunken words could be clearly understood by the Danes, who had a good knowledge of the German language. On these occasions dead silence was maintained in the shed until the danger had passed.

The airplane's assembly was not completed until June 21, a Saturday. Sneum and Petersen had hoped to try to take off shortly before midnight on the twentieth. (At this time of year there is not enough darkness in Denmark to reduce objects on the horizon to silhouettes, providing the sky is clear.) But a German 37-mm antiaircraft battery had rumbled southward along the road near the shed. Had they gone aloft at that time they almost certainly would have been shot down since powerful searchlights accompanied the truck-borne guns.

Foot-high turnip tops fringed the nubby field outside the hangar. The next area was knee-high in barley, but a third field with only a stubble of stiff grass would be fine for the take-off—once the plane had been taxied across the turnips and through the barley.

Their mechanic having returned to Copenhagen, it was agreed that Andersen would give them a helping hand in the final phase. Before take-off the fliers had some ticklish flight problems to consider.

During previous weeks, they had obtained considerable quantities of fuel for the projected flight, something which could still be done in Denmark at that time without enormous difficulty. This fuel was in fifty cans stacked behind the seats in the plane's cabin, making the craft unduly heavy.

Power lines which were strung across the far end of the take-off field would be serious obstacles. Sneum, who would be at the controls, decided he would try to make the craft airborne about midway down the field, where it dipped slightly, and would then have to gauge quickly whether he could fly over the wires. If not, the chance of flying under them would have to be taken—a very risky maneuver.

Timing also would have to be perfect. The fliers knew that an express train roared by the field every night shortly before midnight. Their take-off should coincide with the passage of the train so that its rumble would drown out the noise of the plane's engine. There had been no possibility of smoothing over any areas of the take-off area for fear of German detection although both fliers had surveyed the fields as thoroughly as they could on several occasions.

Although the resistance movement against the Nazis was developing rapidly at that time and illegal radio sets were being operated, the fliers had refrained from having the underground convey any information of their proposed flight to the Allies. There was too much danger of German detection or a possible leak in other quarters.

Aerial gauntlet

Shortly after 10:00 P.M., June 21, Sneum and Petersen held a last, hurried conference with Andersen at his dwelling over coffee and sandwiches. Then they donned their uniforms and put their civilian clothes over them, appearing almost comically bulky in this garb. Sneum had in his possession detailed maps of Denmark but the only map of Britain and surrounding waters had been torn from an atlas. It was a quite unsatisfactory map for such a flight, a voyage of some five hundred miles across the westerly portion of Denmark and the North Sea before they could reach any part of eastern England or Scotland.

These preparations completed, the fliers and Andersen quietly proceeded to the shed. Luckily, the night was clear, a slight summer breeze whispering through the trees and across the grassland.

As quietly as they could, the men opened the doors of the shed about one hour before midnight. Carefully they pulled the craft out of its shelter. The span of the wings somewhat exceeded that of the door and several hard shoves were needed to get it through. The tips of the wings were damaged and torn during this operation but there was no time for any repairs.

Sneum climbed into the cockpit and took over the controls. Glancing over his shoulder he saw the pile of reserve fuel cans, the siphon hose which would be used to feed this fuel into the regular tanks and a broomstick and a white towel they would need later. Remembering that the plane's tanks had been nearly empty for more than a year, Sneum speculated uneasily on whether or not resin in the evaporating fuel had gummed up the fuel filters. Nothing else had been placed aboard—not even food—so as not to add any weight.

Faint sounds of thick German voices and the sudden, heavier noise of a Wehrmacht vehicle clattering along a lane carried across the cool, night air. For a few minutes there was no sound except Petersen's quick breathing as he turned over the propeller to lubricate and prime the aircraft's engine.

Sneum tightened his safety belt across his lap. Keld Petersen, revolver tucked in his belt, waited nervously in front of the craft. Then from a distance came the unmistakable rumble of an approaching train.

"Now! Contact!" Sneum said in a low but distinct voice.

Keld reached up with both hands, grasped the edge of the propeller and flipped it down sharply. As the train neared

the bottom of the take-off field, the Gypsy engine broke
into a roar that, to the fliers at least, seemed to rip the night
apart. Poul Andersen crouched and pulled away the chocks
which had been placed in front of the wheels. Keld, pistol
in hand, was already running clumsily across the turnips,
trying not to stumble over the rough dirt clods, leading
OY-DOK toward the barley field.

Sneum worked the throttle, certain that the nearby Germans could not fail to hear the racket of the engine. He had
hoped that the train would sound even louder than it did.

Keld ran on, waving his pistol, breathing hard, his face
taut and sweating. If the Germans came now, he was determined to empty his revolver against them and then go after
them with his bare hands until he was killed or knocked unconscious. Perhaps this would permit Sneum to escape and
give warning to Andersen. All the men knew that the fliers
could expect no mercy if they were caught.

Fortunately, the engine of the plane worked smoothly, apparently as good as new.

Running ahead across the barley field as a guide to
Sneum, Keld glanced over his shoulder. The propeller fanned
the barley, pulling the aircraft roughly through the thick
growth. Petersen saw the crudely mended tail rise up and
then thud down again. He quickly glanced right and left.
The silhouettes of German sentries and some other soldiers
were visible beyond a fringe of trees and shrubbery but none
of them seemed suspicious of any unusual event taking place.

In the distance sparks spurted from the train's wheels and
its engineer sounded one long, lugubrious toot as the express pounded through the night. To Petersen and Sneum
the noise of the plane sounded louder than that of a bomber.

Upon reaching the edge of the barley field where the
grassland began, Petersen doubled back to the plane a short
distance behind him, and scrambled into the cockpit, muttering "everything good, so far." Sneum opened the throttle
and the little plane shot forward. In front of them were the

power lines between two poles on either side of the open
field.

Sneum pulled back hard on the control stick and the plane
nosed upward. Suddenly Sneum, who had been silently concentrating on his nerve-wracking job, shouted: "I don't
think we can clear those wires. Hang on."

Inwardly taut as a violin string but outwardly calm,
Sneum pushed the control stick forward and the plane's nose
dipped. Petersen had the sensation of hunching his shoulders
and involuntarily ducked his head as they flew under the
power lines.

Sneum drew hard on the stick again and once more the
ship began to climb, seeming to drag its wheels across the
sloping field and over the cab of the railway locomotive. In
the locomotive's cab, less than twenty feet below, one of
the engineers happened to look up and saw the plane. The
fliers perceived everything below clearly but made no farewell gestures.

The German soldiers spotted the small aircraft hedge-
hopping somewhat like an artillery spotting plane. In the
monochromatic light the white crosses that quartered the red
fields of the Danish flags made them appear somewhat like
the Luftwaffe's Maltese Cross. The Germans must have
thought so because they did not open fire of any kind.

The plane, now doing some ninety miles an hour, barely
skimmed over a grove of trees and then, rising higher,
banked westward. Although it was off the ground, these
initial moments were particularly tense ones for the fliers
since this was actually the first real test of its flying ability.
It might still stall or sideslip into a crash at any moment,
especially if one of the aileron or rudder wires should mal-
function or snap.

"How does she fly?" Keld asked anxiously.

"Left wing heavy," Sneum replied. "The angles of inci-
dence are all wrong and the nose pulls down."

From the shadow of the shed Poul Andersen watched the
craft until it became a tiny speck against the vast dome of

the sky and then vanished. Then he silently returned to his
dwelling.

Shortly after swinging westward, Sneum followed a railway track to check the plane's compass. In that direction it
read thirty degrees off. Because they had no radio, they
would have no way of knowing in advance if they were
being intercepted. Their slow speed made it possible for
even a rifleman to bring them down or seriously disable
them with a few lucky shots. Sneum, however, had carefully chartered their course so that it would avoid German
military posts, airfields, or troop concentrations.

An airfield control tower saw the biplane flying over the
Little Belt between Fyn and Jutland. The base flashed
searchlight instructions to the craft to land, but the pilots
did not reply by wagging their wings and coming down.
They were at three thousand feet at that time and boring
into a huge cloud bank. Their only blind flying instrument
was a turn and bank indicator. Near Haderslev, just across
the Little Belt, they came out of the clouds and piloted a
zigzag course, hoping to cross the coast between the islands
of Fano and Romo.

The Fano radar station picked up the aircraft and vec-
tored a fighter into the air, but the Luftwaffe pilot was unable to find the small plane in the night skies.

Back at Elsesminde, Andersen phoned various friends living along the Jutland coast to the west whether they had
heard of any strange aircraft being brought down. No such
report had materialized. Shortly after 1:30 A.M., June 22,
Andersen went to bed. No German soldiers came to bother
him.

The plane's nose still tended to dip and Sneum had to
keep the stick sharply back. Occasionally the craft yawed
sickeningly. As soon as they had a chance the pilots took off
their civilian outer clothing. There were no instrument lights
in the machine so Petersen directed his flashlight on the dials
until their radium-tinted needles absorbed enough light to

glow for about fifteen minutes. Gasoline fumes from loosely capped cans filled the cabin.

The fliers crossed the western coast of Denmark in the early morning hours. When they had been flying steadily over the sea for about an hour the motor began spluttering. The flashlight showed that the oil pressure gauge was giving no reading. Sneum had to throttle full back, then go down into a sharp glide. He feared that the carburetors had temporarily iced up in the somewhat cold upper air and hoped that warmer air lower down might resolve this trouble.

There was nothing to do but hope for the best. There were no parachutes and no lifejackets or small inflatable raft aboard.

A few hundred feet above the water the engine suddenly caught. Sneum threw forward the throttle, pulled back the control stick and at last they began to roar upward. The flashlight showed that their oil pressure was between zero and five gallons.

After some four hours of flight their fuel tank was almost empty. This plane was not designed for any long flights. Petersen was groggy from the fuel fumes and Sneum told him to reach over and take the control stick. Then he opened the port-side cabin door and, as wind howled into the airplane, he took the siphon hose and warily stepped out onto the wing, holding on to the cockpit door with one hand.

Groping along the smooth fuselage, Sneum took anxious minutes to find the fuel filler cap, unscrew it, and fit the hose into the cap as the plane wobbled in the air. Then he returned to the cabin, took the control stick with one hand and held the door slightly ajar so as not to crush the hose.

One tin at a time, sloshing the liquid everywhere and completely drenching Sneum, Petersen began funneling fuel into the hose and pumping it into the tank. When the tank was full, Sneum again had to go out on the wing to detach the hose. The possibility of having the hose permanently fixed to the tank via a hole in the door had been considered

before the take-off, but the men decided against it, one of
the reasons being that such a connection would hamper the
pilot in the critical early phase of flight.

By the position of the North Star they could tell they were
on course. Dawn on Sunday, June 22, came bright and cloud-
less, the North Sea glittering in the morning sun.

About six hours after their take-off, the two fliers saw
two pairs of fighter planes racing sleekly toward them—
British Royal Air Force Hurricanes and Spitfires. The four
fighters heeled to make passes at the mysterious craft, cir-
cling around OY-DOK at hundreds of miles an hour. They
orbited closer and closer, apparently to have a better look
at the red and white flags and the somewhat unfamiliar identification letters. Sneum, keeping his craft headed in the general direction of Britain, shouted:

"Quick, Keld, show them the white towel!"

Petersen hastily knotted the big white towel over the
broomstick and thrust it through the window next to him.
He waved it frantically and the four fighters slipped past
and winged out of sight.

Shortly thereafter a small island hove into view.

Petersen who was attentively scanning the map shouted:

"No sign of any such island on the map, this looks like
the mouth of the Zuider Zee [Holland]! Do you think we
could be way off course?"

"Could very well be," Sneum said, grinning in spite of
his uneasiness. "That map is nothing wonderful, you know,
and we have been flying blind to say the least."

What they hoped to be Scotland was actually Coquet Island, a tiny spot not shown on their map. It lies close to the
English shore, southeast of Berwick, which is about sixty
miles southeast of Edinburgh.

The plane flew on, Sneum and Petersen busily looking for
a landing spot along the mainland coast. Nosing the plane
down, they neared a small coastal town. They perceived
that no one seemed to be moving around in the town. They

did not know it but an air raid had been sounded below when their craft had been sighted. Seeing soldiers in a camp below, the two Danes decided it was best to land in a hurry before British antiaircraft guns opened up against them.

At his farm, back in Denmark, Poul had risen, eaten breakfast and was taking care of his cows. He tuned in on the British Broadcasting Company hoping to hear some news about the plane but nothing of the kind was mentioned.

Gracefully, the tiny ship glided downward toward a broad, open field devoid of trees, telegraph poles, or fences. The plane landed somewhat heavily and rolled to a stop near a gate in a fence at the end of the field. Sneum and Petersen, their faces haggard, smelling strongly of gasoline, stepped out of the plane with sighs of relief.

At that moment a Northumberland farmer ran through the gate and toward the plane, a pitchfork in his hand. He was obviously somewhat frightened.

When one of the men asked him politely, "What place is this?" he remained silent and looked nervously at the plane.

"At least can you tell us if it's England or Scotland?" the officer asked, both of his queries couched in good English.

"England!" the farmer shouted over his shoulder, as he ran off to get help.

He returned shortly with an armed member of the Home Guard on a bicycle, a sprinkling of soldiers and airmen, some civilians, and an armored car.

The Britons, soon satisfied that the two fliers were indeed escaped Danes, escorted them to the RAF station at Acklington.

Here they told their story in full, to the considerable amazement of assembled British officers. After partaking of a hearty breakfast, the flying escapees were told they would be sent the following day to London's clearing center for foreign troops who entered Britain unconventionally. Then they were told to go to sleep.

Within five days of their landing Sneum was taken from the London clearing center for special assignment and Keld was commissioned in the Royal Air Force. The film of Fano and other information the fliers had proved extremely valuable to the Allies.

At about 8:00 A.M. on Sunday, June 22, Poul Andersen telephoned the Odense police that his dismantled airplane had been stolen. Fortunately, a Luftwaffe pilot from a nearby base had deserted a few days previous. When the Danish police informed the local Nazi authorities, the latter apparently believed that the pilot might have stolen the plane. The police did not emphasize the fact—which they knew—that the plane supposedly was completely dismantled and unable to fly.

In about a week, however, the Nazi authorities became suspicious and investigated Andersen. By that time Poul had heard a report on the BBC broadcasts beamed on Denmark that two Danish airmen had arrived in England. Neither of the men's names nor the details of their escape were related. In Britain newspapers were not permitted to mention the story.

Andersen stoutly maintained that he knew absolutely nothing about the affair, that he had never reassembled the plane and that as far as he knew the craft was still in the shed up to the dawn of Sunday, the twenty-second. Perhaps some local Danes had stolen it to sell as junk, he added.

The Germans were not quite satisfied and kept close watch on the farmer but they learned nothing further. They kept him under surveillance for more than a year, preventing Andersen during that period from helping the Danish underground organizations in any way. Later in the war Poul helped the underground in various ways but never as spectacularly as in the case of Sneum and Petersen.

Sneum was one of the first two Allied agents to return to Denmark by plane, being dropped by parachute at a predesignated spot. They brought a portable wireless transmitter with them. In Copenhagen they met Arne Duus-Hansen, a radio engineer, who helped them broadcast their first message to England. After several months, however, Sneum's presence in Denmark was detected by the Germans—who were then becoming much harsher toward the rebellious Danes—and he fled on foot across the frozen Sound to Sweden in early 1943.

Keld Petersen served honorably in the RAF, participating in many operations. This author does not know whether Petersen is still alive today but knows that Sneum still is, an active advertising executive, working and residing in Switzerland.

The whole episode ended happily for stouthearted Poul Andersen. After the war the British manufacturers of the De Havilland plane presented him with a brand-new replica of the craft which had been stolen from him.

SMORREBROD

The vigil

The three men in the darkened room tensed expectantly as the hands of their wrist watches merged at twelve and the day of November 3, 1944, was tolled into memory by the big clock of Aalborg's Saint Budolfi Cathedral.

The room was under the eaves of a somewhat dilapidated two-story house on a hill in the outskirts of the ancient Danish city in northern Jutland.

All three men had entered the house about one hour before midnight, coming from different points in the city. They had arrived furtively, on foot, and at spaced intervals. Each was bundled up in a muffler, woollen cap, winter suit and overcoat, for the night was bitingly cold, the city and its environs snow-whitened.

The men did not carry arms. Danes caught with arms on their persons could expect the worst from the Germans. In a battered leather case carried under his overcoat one of the trio carried equipment which would be of special importance after midnight—a powerful pair of binoculars.

All three had hugged the shadows of buildings and trees as they proceeded through the city and up the hill road leading to the house. Each quickened his pace when obliged to cross an open area, sometimes running, eyes darting from side to side, halting briefly for a panting rest when reaching another pool of shadow. Before leaving shadow areas, they scanned all areas within eyeshot. Sometimes their eyes flicked nervously at nearby windows or doors. There grave peril could lurk—possibly a pro-Nazi Dane near a telephone, or, more probably, a *Gestapo* agent. The city was eerily quiet in the winter starlight, windows shuttered, no lights visible. A strict curfew and black-out were in effect and German patrols were on the prowl, on foot, in automobiles and on motorcycles.

The three men were top fighters in the Danish resistance campaign in Jutland. The owner of the hilltop house had been advised of their coming and promptly ushered them in after a muttered exchange of greetings. He knew who they were, notably the slim man with the keen eyes and the determined jaw. This was Jens Toldstrup, whose real name was Anton Jensen, a customs official of Aalborg and a lieutenant in the Danish Army reserve. As far as the Germans were concerned he was the most wanted man in northern Jutland, leader of the entire resistance movement in that area.

After all of them had arrived, Toldstrup turned to the owner of the building, a minor but trustworthy underground helper.

"Something hot is on the griddle tonight. You will know all about it soon enough," the resistance leader said. "Mount guard for us there"—he pointed to a window next to the main door, now closed—"and keep an eye on that road. Report anything suspicious immediately. Now, where do we go upstairs?"

The landlord, his face a blur in the darkness, nodded his agreement to these instructions and replied:

"There, to your right is the stairway. Watch your step. It is a bit rickety and the banister is weak in spots. Go up two flights and turn to your left. The room is at the end of the hall on the right. There are three chairs and a couch in the room so you will not be too uncomfortable. If I have to shout a warning you will hear me clearly—and the same goes for you."

The man then turned to a nearby table and picked up a platter loaded with sandwiches and a bottle.

"Take this food and this brandy. This is no time to go hungry," he added. "And remember, in case of a bad emergency there is a back door. You can see it over there beyond the staircase. It is unlatched. From it a narrow path leads to a low brick wall with trees and streets beyond. I can always latch it after you have gone and stall anyone in pursuit as long as I can."

The three resistance men thanked him for his foresight and then climbed upstairs in silence, guided by a flashlight which Toldstrup held low and shaded with one hand. Entering the room, Toldstrup snapped off the flashlight. The single window gave sufficient light for the men to get their bearings.

"Now, let's get set," Toldstrup said, partially opening one half of the small paned window. "Bring up the chairs close to the window. Not too close—yes, that's fine. Our heads will be just above the level of the window sill."

The chairs in place, the men sat down. Toldstrup removed the binoculars from their case, clapped them to his eyes, and beamed them on the area visible through the window. The eyes of the others followed his.

"Everything looks pretty quiet over there, just sentries going their rounds and a man walking toward a low building," Toldstrup said. "He's probably going to the latrine. Maybe it will be his last such trip, at least I hope so."

"Yes, if everything goes well," one of his companions replied. "We don't really know what has happened to our man. A lot depends on that, although chemically things may be okay."

"Well, let's wait and see," Toldstrup replied. "He has a stout heart. Midnight is near and we'll soon know."

The window offered an excellent view of part of the city and its environs on this clear night. The trio was not scanning the city. Their eyes were directed at a flat area covered with various types of buildings and towers, outside the city and about a mile and a half distant from the watching men.

The zone could be fairly well perceived with the naked eye, but the binoculars were needed to bring it into truly sharp focus. This was the big German Luftwaffe airdrome, formerly the municipal flying field of Aalborg, at the time a vital aerial communications link between the Reich and occupied Denmark and Norway.

Toldstrup and his two lieutenants were awaiting their own kind of zero hour—the culmination of one of the most daring and shrewdly plotted sabotage operations of World War II. The sight they hoped to see would rival anything in a movie spectacular. There also was a good possibility that nothing at all might happen, there being two ticklish factors involved—one human, the other chemical.

If everything went well the big airdrome, with its fifty-odd fighter planes, its staff of some two hundred Luftwaffe officers and men, its hangars and barracks would be an inferno in the early hours of November 4, 1944.

All preparations had gone smoothly except for one serious occurrence at the eleventh hour.

Toldstrup's key agent on the field—one of a number of Danish workers employed there by the Germans during daytime hours—had been arrested while carrying out last-minute orders and held for questioning.

The arrest occurred shortly after 1:00 P.M., November 2. The resistance leaders had learned of the arrest but beyond that, nothing.

Midnight came and went. Nothing happened on the airfield, nothing at all. No bang, no flash, no smoke. Doubt began to bite deep into the minds of the trio. But they stubbornly maintained their vigil.

It would be much longer than expected.

The lunchless men

Jutland resistance leaders had discussed the possibility of a major strike at the airfield on various occasions during the previous months, only to pigeonhole the idea as not feasible.

Security precautions at the airfield, one of the most important Nazi installations in Denmark, were at maximum pitch day and night. It was surrounded by electrically charged barbed wire, guards at the gates and on patrol around the clock.

True, some thirty Danish mechanics and other workmen were employed on the field during daylight hours. But these were meticulously frisked coming and going. Infiltration of saboteurs by night was virtually impossible. The records of any Danes applying for work there or summoned to do it were checked exhaustively by the Germans.

The underground had not been able to infiltrate a trusted saboteur among the Danish airfield workers until late October. The hope that a big coup could be organized against the airdrome remained steadfast, however, fanned by Allied victories in Europe and elsewhere.

Then, in October, a development occurred which provided Toldstrup with the Archilles' heel or perhaps better a Trojan horse, which the underground needed.

In a village near Aalborg one of Toldstrup's men, looking for active and able recruits for expanding resistance operations, met a man named Jens Christensen. Christensen was a skilled mechanic who had been forced by the Germans to work for them in a small factory near Aalborg.

In conversing with the resistance man Christensen told him that he hated the Nazis, as virtually all Danes did.

"We need men like you, with special skills," the resistance man said. "Would you be willing to work for us? Are you willing to face the danger?"

"Absolutely. I have had it up to here with these swine," Christensen said, placing his right hand under his chin in an expressive gesture. "Thus far they have nothing against me, at least nothing that they could prove. That may be an advantage in my case. Of course, here and there I have done my bit. You know, the usual, approving machinery which I knew was defective, being slow on the job whenever I could, helping some friends hide, and the like.

"Unfortunately, I have had no experience in major sabotage. But I can learn. I am ready to do anything you ask of me. I know engines and machinery of various types very well. I could even qualify as a skilled aviation mechanic if that would be of any help. Perhaps you could give me some explosives and I could go to work in the plant where I am working. Then help me get elsewhere. I know you will protect my family as best you can, whatever happens."

His questioner said that such sabotage was a possibility but that he would like to confer with his colleagues in the underground before taking any action in this matter.

At that time Allied airmen were stepping up their secret parachute drops of ammunition, explosives and other supplies to the Danes. The underground could therefore supply an adequate amount of explosives to Jens if needed.

Both men parted with a friendly handshake after Christensen had informed the other of various places where he could be contacted without arousing suspicion.

On the following day the recruiter saw Toldstrup and told him of the meeting, emphasizing that he had full confidence in the man. Christensen's background was promptly checked. He had spoken the truth about his forced labor. Outside of this obligatory work—something imposed on many Danes—he had not been friendly toward or aided the enemy in any fashion.

In a few days Christensen and Toldstrup met secretly at night in a room above a small café in Aalborg used as an underground meeting place.

"I am quite ready to provide you with explosives but I

think you can be more useful to us elsewhere than in your plant," Toldstrup said over sandwiches and beer. "There are bigger jobs we can tackle—jobs which will really hurt the supermen. Would you be ready to quit your present job and ask the Germans to employ you elsewhere? We will see to it that your wife and two children are immediately moved secretly to some safer area if circumstances demand it."

"I will go anywhere and do anything you want me to do. I am determined now to risk all for my country," Jens replied quietly. "I will fabricate some argument to convince my bosses that I should be shifted if you want me to go elsewhere."

Toldstrup, convinced of the man's sincerity, then bade him farewell and told him that he would receive instructions within a few days and should go on as usual until then.

During the next twenty-four hours the resistance leader and his aides again turned their thoughts to the airdrome. There was no question that it was the prime target in the Aalborg area, which is about 120 miles northwest of Copenhagen, on the Lim Fjord.

Via secret radio sets the Danes could request an Allied bombing of the field, but they knew this would be a suicidal affair. The field was backed by numerous antiaircraft and radar installations. It had its own fighter plane complement, pilots ready to take off in a flash. Searchlights would immediately pinpoint any night attackers.

The problem facing the resistance commanders at Aalborg was to get sufficient explosives into the airfield area, equipped with timing devices. But how? Confident that they would find a way, the resistance leaders decided that they would instruct Christensen to try and get assigned to the airdrome as a mechanic.

On October 15 Christensen succeeded, by stressing his skills as an aviation mechanic and proving his record was excellent as far as the Nazis were concerned.

Reporting to Toldstrup in Aalborg after his first day's work, Christensen was not optimistic. German security there was just about perfect, he emphasized. At most, he said, he might smash a few things with a crowbar or make some machinery defective. Causing any large-scale damage without explosives seemed out of the question.

"The morning and evening frisking at the gates is as thorough as ever, pockets inside out every time, shoes, hats, socks all checked," he said. "There are two good things, however. I have obtained a very good idea of the general layout and made a rough pencil map for you stressing points of particular interest to us. Also I have contacted two Danes on the field who indicated they would be ready to work for us. I believe they are trustworthy. They will visit you tomorrow for checking. But even if they prove okay, Anton, that will mean a mere six hands at work, hands without explosives. That's not much. Something else will have to be done."

Christensen then drew his map from his pocket and handed it to Toldstrup.

"That's fine, Jens," Toldstrup said. "Quite precise and clear, better than anything we have right now on this. Let us now part for today and I will seek a solution to the explosives problem."

The following day the two other men were interviewed, deemed trustworthy, and instructed to obey Christensen's orders. True, none of the men was an experienced saboteur but this factor would have to be taken in stride. At least an underground cell had been established on the airfield during the daytime.

That day Toldstrup and several of his aides discussed the entire problem at length. Three major questions confronted them.

1. Considerable quantities of explosives would have to be stored in the airdrome area and only three men were available for this.

2. If the men were given explosives they would have to smuggle them in somehow over a number of days until sufficient amounts were available for a big blasting.

3. The explosives would have to be camouflaged as something else—something the agents could bring in without being suspected and hide till the moment was ripe for attack.

"There must be some loophole, something the Nazis do not suspect," Toldstrup said. "I have not seen any of these workmen close at hand as they near the gates in the morning or leave in the evening. Have any of you studied them? Can you think of anything that might be helpful?"

"Yes, I have seen them on various occasions," one of his aides replied. "Now let me think a moment. Ah! yes, yes, there is something. Something they bring to the airfield every day and do not bring out at night. Very commonplace at that. Luncheon food. You can guess what it is, ah! you're grinning. . . ."

"Oh! Of course, *smorrebrod!*" Toldstrup said, his eyes glinting. "Possibly this is not checked by the Germans. Perhaps, gentlemen, we can build a fine Trojan horse out of something that is not what it appears to be."

That night Toldstrup saw Christensen again and told him of the result of the earlier conference.

"Ah! By Almighty God, this might work," Christensen said. "The Nazis do not check this. They did originally, I believe, and then it became all too time-consuming and apparently futile so they gave it up. I can guess your idea. It will be a bit of hardship on us three but we'll survive. A little more on our breakfast plates, that's all."

Toldstrup then got men from one of his special explosives units to help in the plan. Using plastic explosives, the underground workers began preparing small bombs in the form of paper covered parcels about eight-inches square and two-and-a-half-inches thick.

These were given to Christensen and his two aides at the rate of three packages a day. Every morning the three workers carried these packages openly past the German guards, one per man. This aroused no suspicion. Every other Danish workman employed on the field arrived there in the morning carrying a similar parcel, sometimes wrapped with string, sometimes not.

This was *smorrebrod* which in Danish means open sandwich, a word widely applied to any type of luncheon food carried by Danish workmen to their jobs.

Storing the bombs in the airfield was chancy but Toldstrup had suggested to the three men that they do this in their clothing lockers. The biggest danger in this was that the explosives gave forth a somewhat unusual, heavy odor. However, barring a sweeping German search of the locker area, this storing phase should proceed smoothly. Fortunately, other workers were seldom in this room, using the lockers mainly to store extra clothing which they used from time to time. Usually they ate their lunch in the work area to which they had been assigned. Christensen also decided to keep the windows open as long as possible to weaken the odor of the explosives.

For more than a fortnight the trio ate no lunches. No one noticed this. If any other Danes perceived it they kept their mouths shut.

During this period they smuggled in some fifty high-explosive bombs and twenty incendiary bombs.

On November 2 Toldstrup informed Christensen and his two aides that sufficient explosives were now on the airfield. The following day they were to plant their lethal seeds.

At noontime the next day the trio had plenty to do instead of idling around during the lunch hour. They wandered here and there separately, seemingly just having a look around. Toldstrup had explained carefully to them how to crush the thin copper ends of the time pencils which would arm the bombs. These delay fuses worked chemically and were supposed to set off the explosives after twelve hours had elapsed.

Proceeding to the locker room at different intervals in an unhurried manner, the three saboteurs filled their pockets with as many bombs as they could carry. Then they fanned out, going from hangar to hangar and to various other buildings, placing explosives in the engines or cockpits of aircraft and setting incendiary charges in gasoline and oil dumps. Each ostentatiously carried various tools in his hands, so that if they were questioned they could claim they were fulfilling some work assignment in this or that area.

As soon as one batch of explosives had been planted the men returned to the locker room and picked up more of them.

One of the men strolled into the Luftwaffe main barracks, blandly informing a guard there that he had been instructed to perform some emergency repairs to a leaking water pipe. The gullible guard let him in and the saboteur went to work. He made a hole in one of the walls, seemingly looking for a defective pipe, and put something from his pockets into it. Several incendiaries also were placed in other areas where their detection was unlikely.

Alleging that he was seeking a certain officer to make an urgent report, Christensen got into the officers' mess. He was told that the officer was not there, something he had made sure of beforehand. As he left the building he succeeded in placing an explosive in a trash basket which, he believed, would not be cleaned out until the late morning of the following day.

Bombs also were placed alongside one of the main water pipes, a vital conduit for any fire-fighting operations. On the field was a mobile workshop full of very special tools brought from Germany. The Luftwaffe was so afraid that this vehicle might be damaged by sabotage or Allied bombing that it was driven off the airdrome every night to be hidden in a safer place. One of Christensen's aides managed to enter it unobserved, the German guard watching over it having carelessly taken time out for lunch. When the Dane left his pockets were lighter.

Shortly after 1:00 P.M. Christensen returned alone to the locker room and picked up the last bomb. Before placing it in a pocket of his overalls, he swiftly but carefully washed out the lockers with sharp-smelling soap and water. Some odds and ends of clothing, tobacco, cigarettes, and some towels were left in the three lockers. Totally empty they might arouse suspicion. He had opened the windows when he arrived in the morning and they were still open at this time.

Leaving the locker room, Christensen wandered into an empty office building. Its tenants were probably having lunch at that moment. He had planted his explosive and was heading for the main door when he heard footsteps. A German officer strode in. Jens was lighting his pipe with outward calm, gazing detachedly at some pictures of Luftwaffe planes and pin-up photographs of pretty girls culled from German magazines. His nerves were jumping, however, when the officer shouted angrily:

"Hey, what are you doing here, you have no business here. *Donnerwetter!* Speak up, man!"

"Oh, really nothing at all, nothing at all," the Dane replied, removing his pipe from his mouth, and speaking in German, of which he had a good knowledge. "Just strolling around during my lunch hour. I had heard there were some nice pictures here and wanted to look at them, Herr Offizier. No harm in that, is there?" The officer did not cease frowning.

"Where do you work, in what capacity?" he snapped.

"I am an aviation mechanic, mostly assigned to hangar number two," the Dane said, removing his cap and adopting a very respectful air. "My record is in order. I am new here but they know all about me. I am permitted to walk around during lunchtime. I was just curious. That's all, Herr Offizier."

"You're lying, you damned Dane," the officer shouted. "We'll see about this. Consider yourself under arrest, right now. Hey, guard, over here, on the double."

A nearby guard ran up and seized Christensen by the arm, threatening him with his tommy gun. Then the Dane, harried by gloomy forebodings but happy that the last bomb had been planted, was led away for questioning.

During hours of interrogation Jens stood firm, monotonously repeating: "I was just curious, that's all. I know of no espionage or sabotage." Punches to the stomach and the mouth and dire threats of all kinds could not break him.

After the questioning he was hustled to a guardhouse, informed that he was being held for further examination on the following day. There was one good thing about being in the guardhouse—the building was at some distance from any point where explosives had been secreted.

His two aides had heard that he had been arrested and were alarmed. Would he talk? Would he break down? Confess something? Just a few words—the Nazis were pastmasters at wringing words from prisoners—would be enough.

Both men discussed the advisability of trying to leave the field at once on some excuse or other but realized this would be foolhardy, possibly creating suspicion and, in turn, their arrest. They decided the only thing to do was to get on with their work, mask their jittery nerves, and leave at the end of the day as if everything was normal.

At dusk they and the other Danish workers left the airfield after being carefully searched as usual. After darkness had fallen, the two saboteurs hastened to Toldstrup's headquarters in Aalborg. They reported the arrest immediately. All the explosives, including the incendiaries, had been carefully planted with the exception, perhaps, of the one carried by Christensen on his ill-fated final trip.

"We believe he did succeed in planting it," one of the men said. "If it had been found on his person the Nazis undoubtedly would have created a big stink and seized all of us without more ado."

"Do you think Christensen talked?" Toldstrup said gravely.

"We don't know about that," one of them replied. "Now, what happens to us? Even if he doesn't talk and the bombs begin to go off we don't want to be around here."

"You are quite right. You must get out of here and I will see to it," Toldstrup answered.

Within an hour, they were secretly sped out of Aalborg
to a remote coastal spot in a motor-driven fishing craft.
Here they lodged with an underground sympathizer, told to
remain in hiding until further notice.

Nightmare at dawn

A few days prior to these events, Toldstrup and two of
his principal aides decided that the house on the hill would
be a good vantage point to await developments when the
time came. They knew that the owner was a good patriot,
and duly contacted him by phone, their conversation couched
in veiled terms. He told them there was a room upstairs
with an excellent view of the airfield. It was agreed that
they would visit the house soon, the exact time to be established by another phone call.

This call was made about 9:00 P.M. on the night of the
third. The three resistance leaders proceeded to the house
to watch the airfield.

The morning hours of November 4 dragged on slowly,
endlessly in the upstairs room, the men, singly and in turn,
taking catnaps on the bed. Two, three, four, five A.M.
Situation unchanged—no bang or flash.

After 4:00 A.M. they informed the landlord that he could
go to bed, that they would arouse him if necessary.

The sun came up and still the routine on the airdrome
seemed normal. If the Germans had found out anything,
they had carried out their search at night and had everything under control. Just a few of the Luftwaffe men were
emerging from buildings and walking around or proceeding
to other structures. There was no confusion, no hurry.

When the sun rose the hopes of the three men in the
room had dropped almost to zero. All hell should have
broken out by now. Something had gone wrong. Christensen must have been tortured during the night and forced
to reveal the whereabouts of the bombs and these had been
duly neutralized. Weeks of preparation amid constant dan-

ger nullified, the prospect of ever attempting it again almost hopeless, Toldstrup and his aides reflected sadly.

Christensen, his mouth blood-clotted, his midriff still aching from the punches, had also been awake throughout most of the night hours. The Dane had been placed in a small room with a barred window and an armed guard outside the locked door. At 8:00 P.M. he was given some thin gruel and a slice of bread. He had virtually given up hope of anything happening as the sun's rays stabbed through the barred window. What the devil had gone wrong? Were the bombs defective in some way? Had their noontime movements been spotted and the explosives found and disarmed? Had his two companions been seized and blabbed?

Christensen had one consolation the others did not have— he knew that he at least had divulged nothing.

About half an hour after sunrise, Toldstrup and his companions, their faces drawn, crestfallen, decided that they had better abandon their vigil and return to the city.

Then, just as Toldstrup was taking a final look through the binoculars, all three could hear a bang on the field.

"It's working. It's taking place!" Toldstrup shouted excitedly, slapping his knee with his left hand. "There goes one of the Luftwaffe planes, the whole business, up in the air, and falling down, flaming wreckage."

"Yes, the bombs are working!" his two friends shouted in unison.

"Oh, Fatso Goering, here goes some of your precious Luftwaffe," Toldstrup exclaimed. "Here, you fellows look through the glasses. We'll take turns at them. There's going to be a lot to see."

Then another plane came apart at the seams, spewing wreckage all around, wreathed in smoke and flame. And another and another as building after building were ripped by detonations. The blasts were simultaneous or occurred so close together that they formed almost one continuous booming on the airfield. Germans, some in their night clothes, poured out of buildings in confusion bordering on panic,

DENMARK   *149*

obviously not quite knowing what to do, caught completely
by surprise. Fire engines raced madly around the field trying to put out blazes, but as soon as they got one partially
under control another would break out and burn fiercely
elsewhere.

Jubilation reigned in the room under the roof of the hilltop house, the men slapping each other on the back and
taking turns at the binoculars or just keeping their eyes
riveted on the airdrome.

The owner of the house was awakened with a gleeful
shout down the stairs and hurriedly joined the men above.

"There she goes, the main barracks and the officers' mess.
You see, where the smoke is rising to the right," Toldstrup
reported, gazing through the binoculars. "And another blast,
a good one. That hangar's gone. It's had its morning
smorrebrod. . . ."

Another hangar was wrecked almost at the same moment.
The valuable mobile truck went up with a loud bang, its
equipment shattered beyond repair.

On the airfield Luftwaffe officers, faces blackened by
smoke, some bloody from cuts inflicted by flying glass or
other wreckage, roared frantic orders. Three men rushed
up to a parked aircraft and, as one of them was just about
to reach into the cockpit, the whole machine blew up in their
faces, hurling them yelling and screaming to the ground,
all wounded. Then an officer, determined to do his very best
for Fuehrer and Fatherland, came running from a building
holding one of the *smorrebrod* packages in his hands, one
he had accidentally spotted seconds beforehand. He ran
toward a group of fire fighters. They gave him one look
and, with good intuition, began scattering. But it was too
late. The bomb went off in the officer's hands and he dis-
integrated as the blast also wounded several of the fleeing
fire fighters.

Steadily the pall of smoke over the stricken airfield deepened and pandemonium increased. Several other bombs were
found by Luftwaffe men and carried into the open. They

all went off in their hands, demolishing the bearer and inflicting wounds on others.

The damage to planes was devastating. One, two, three, four, five, up to forty were torn apart, two or three airplanes sometimes being destroyed by the same explosive when they happened to be parked close together.

Toldstrup and his companions could not witness every phase but could imagine what was happening since the general scene left no doubt that hell had broken out.

"Better than a movie spectacular, eh!" one of his aides remarked grinning.

"Great, what a job!" Toldstrup replied. "When Adolf hears about this one he will chew up every carpet in sight!"

The explosions of the bombs stopped after about an hour and a half, but flames licking at one gasoline dump after another caused further detonations and wider fires. The watchers could see stretcher bearers and ambulances going back and forth amid the clouds of smoke, hour after hour.

Toldstrup and his aides remained on the lookout until late in that afternoon, trying to assess as best they could just how much damage had been done. A hurried phone call to an obscure restaurant in Aalborg informed other underground leaders that the coup had caused immense damage.

It was only as winter shadows were lengthening on November 4 that the Germans got the fires under control and succeeded in restoring a semblance of order. Some thirty men were killed or wounded, although these and many other facts only were known later to the Danes in Aalborg. The airdrome would be only partially useful for many weeks, perhaps months. Fires might have been fought more successfully if water had been plentiful but it was not. The bomb placed next to the conduit had done its work.

Reports circulated on November 5 that several German planes sent aloft had exploded in mid-air, all personnel aboard killed by the explosions or falls earthward. Apparently these planes had not been closely checked and for some unknown reason the plastic bombs had been especially tardy in exploding. These reports, however, never were fully verified. They probably occurred at some distance from the field and the Germans never made any admissions that this had happened.

The news that the airfield had been blasted in some mysterious fashion, obviously not an air raid, caused jubilation among Danes in Aalborg. However, they wisely did not demonstrate their glee where Germans or pro-Nazis could see or hear them. On November 4 many hurried to the vicinity of the airfield to observe developments. All were convinced that it was the work of the resistance, but there was wide speculation on how it had been done in view of the known security measures at the field.

At dusk Toldstrup and his companions left the hilltop house after thanking their host for his aid and returned to the city. Here they sought information about what had happened to Christensen but could obtain none. Then they contacted one of the men who had made the bombs. Why had they not gone off around midnight? He stated after some deliberation that the unusual cold had retarded the chemical action of the time pencils, a verdict which eventually was proven correct by experimenting with a similar bomb under the same temperature conditions.

Toldstrup that night sent a wireless message via one of the underground's secret transmitters to London informing the Allies of the day's success. Early the following morning he received a radioed reply stating among other things that . . . YOU COULD NOT HAVE MADE A BETTER ACKNOWLEDGEMENT TO THE ROYAL AIR FORCE FOR THEIR ATTACK ON GESTAPO AARHUS.*

In subsequent days the underground learned details of what had happened to Christensen and how he had refused to make any revelations on the day of his arrest. Shortly

---

* This referred to a daring RAF attack on *Gestapo* headquarters at Aarhus on October 31. The raid had been urged by the Danish underground to destroy *Gestapo* files which would help the Germans in an impending roundup of Danes.

after the blasts began at sunrise, Nazi officers stormed into the prison building and again subjected him to harsh questioning. It did them no good, Christensen insisting that he had gone to the building out of mere curiosity, that he knew nothing about planting bombs or anything like that. The questioning was renewed later in the day with the same results.

The other Danes reported for work, even though they had learned earlier that bombs were wrecking the airfield. It was wiser to do so under the circumstances. They knew the Germans had no real case against them. They had all been checked out the previous day at the regular hour and to accuse them of bringing in large quantities of explosives was just laughable in view of the rigorous frisking at the gates. Luftwaffe officers did grill them as soon as they had been frisked by guards but this led to no arrests. The officers realized that they would need these workers more than ever now, and told them to enter the area to give a helping hand. This the Danes did, as clumsily and as slowly as possible.

Coming up against a wall of silence in Christensen, the Germans sent him to a concentration camp where he spent months of hardship until liberation in the spring of 1945, after V-E Day.

His two airfield aides were never caught by the Nazis and returned to civilian life after the war. The owner of the house on the hill likewise did not fall into Nazi clutches. Toldstrup continued in resistance work till liberation. He lives and works in Denmark today.

For weeks and months after the raid, the Germans speculated on how it had been done but never did get round to the paper packages idea. Details were only known after the war.

4

Norway

Yes, we love with fond devotion
This our land that looms
Rugged, storm-scarred o'er the ocean
With her thousand homes
Love her, in our love recalling
Those who gave us birth
And old tales which night, in falling
Bring as dreams to earth.

*A verse from the Norwegian national anthem
by Björnstjerne Björnson*

ADOLF'S GREATEST
"HORSE"

Moving secretly by sea and air, Hitler's fighting men stabbed at Norway on April 9, 1940, in one of the most astounding Trojan horse operations against a big country in all history. The onslaught against the land of majestic fjords did not proceed as smoothly as the blitz against little Denmark on the same day. Although stunned by the event, the Norwegians fought back with considerable stubbornness into early summer of 1940. Only then could Hitler claim that he really had the country under his paw.

His invasion involved more dirty maneuvers than those used in gobbling up Denmark. So quickly was it carried out, so smoothly were telegraph, train, and other means of communication brought under Nazi control that it was several days before the world realized exactly what had happened.

Gentlemanly King Haakon and his more than three million subjects just could not believe that this could happen in their country.

Norway, one of the most progressive and democratic countries in the world, had enjoyed peace for more than 126 years, her accomplishments in many fields were milestones in human advancement. She had not provoked the Reich in any manner. There was no formal German declaration of war, just a stiff memorandum asking the Norwegians to cooperate in a protective Nazi occupation of the country which the Nazis, as usual, claimed was the target of Allied machinations.

This was flatly refused by the Norwegian government. The memorandum was not submitted prior to the attack as might be presumed. It was presented by the German Minister to Norway, Curt Brauer, to the Norwegian Foreign Office at 4:30 A.M. on April 9. The onslaught was already underway at that time.

German troops were in Norwegian ports or in her territorial waters, hidden below decks, ready to attack as soon as signals and orders were received. Troop transports heading for Oslo Fjord, which twists southward from the capital, were instructed to fly British colors and to respond to any hails in English if such craft came near. Vidkun Quisling, number one Norwegian pro-Nazi and former Defense Minister, and his henchmen were already at work for Hitler when the memorandum was presented.

False or confusing orders were traitorously conveyed to forts, ships, and various military concentrations stipulating that there should be no resistance whatsoever. In some instances these worked and materially helped the German entry.

In spite of the massive surprise, Norwegian fighting ships and coastal artillery took a sharp toll of German seaborne attackers, among other feats sending the cruiser *Bluecher* to the bottom with heavy loss of life.

Hastily assembled Norwegian troops and volunteers fought back bravely near Oslo and at other points for weeks but the odds against them were overwhelming. By June Norwegian armed forces, virtually caught in a sack, had capitulated. A mixed British and French force which had landed in the north to help the Norwegians during the fighting also was defeated and had to be evacuated by sea.

Beloved King Haakon, his son Crown Prince Olav, members of the royal family and members of the legitimate government reluctantly had to flee to England. The King had flatly refused German demarches designed to secure his cooperation with Hitler's New Order in managing the country's affairs. The Nazis promptly attempted an aerial assassination to get him out of the way. Luftwaffe planes sent bombs plummeting into Elverum, in southeastern Norway, a town where the King was in transit. He was not there but the bombs caused considerable damage and inflicted civilian casualties.

There were two major military reasons for Hitler's attack on Norway. Its seizure would provide him with vital coastal bases and harbors and facilitate aerial and naval attacks of all types, principally against Allied naval and merchant shipping. In addition it would ensure continued shipment of Swedish iron ore via the Norwegian sea and other routes to Germany. A grip on Norway and Denmark also would secure his right flank strategically and bolster other nefarious plans being perfected at that very moment: a smashing drive in the following month against Holland, Belgium, France, and the tiny Grand Duchy of Luxembourg, wedged in between Germany and France.

The flight of King Haakon was no callous royal abandonment of the Norwegian people. He and members of his government knew that the Germans would like nothing better than to have them under their hobnailed boots. It was imperative to maintain a legal Norwegian government in London, which could marshal available Norwegian ships and men for the Allies and would constitute a symbol of defiance for true Norwegians everywhere.

People who eventually participated in the Norwegian anti-Nazi underground were given their own special appellation linked with a geographical area where a significant pre-invasion sea incident occurred. It was known as the Altmark affair.

The *Altmark*, an auxiliary supply ship of the German pocket battleship *Graf Spee*, had managed to slip through British blockading craft in waters off Norway in February

1940, heading for Germany. Norwegian naval officers had
made a cursory inspection of the *Altmark* and being satisfied she was unarmed and had nothing suspicious aboard
had cleared her for continued travel to the Reich. Actually
there were three hundred British seamen aboard taken from
ships sunk by the *Graf Spee*. They had been locked in
storerooms and in an empty oil tank, their presence sedu-
lously hidden from the somewhat careless Norwegian inspectors.

The British government knew full well they were aboard.
Churchill, then British First Lord of the Admiralty, personally ordered a British destroyer flotilla to go into Norwegian waters, board the German vessel and liberate the prisoners. On the night of February 16–17 the British destroyer
Cossack caught the *Altmark* hiding in Norway's Joessing
Fjord. A British boarding party swarmed over the *Altmark*
and an affray occurred in which four Germans were killed
and five wounded. The prisoners were then transferred to
the *Cossack* and the destroyer sailed away.

A vehement Norwegian government protest ensued but
Britain replied that Norway itself had violated international
law by allowing its waters to be used by the Germans to
convey British prisoners of war to internment.

After the invasion, the Norwegians began calling any resistant a joessing in commemoration of the incident. It took
hold and was freely applied to both men and women, although "home front" operations were the words applied to
underground activities as a whole.

The incident brought Adolf to the *teppichfresser* (carpet chewer) stage, particularly since his supermen aboard
the *Altmark* had not put up any real fight. The incident
allegedly spurred him noticeably in his plans involving possible seizure of Norway.

On February 21, he called in General Nikolaus von
Falkenhorst, a World War I commander, and told him he
would be placed in command of operations against Norway.

As in Denmark, Hitler saw to it that a military chief was

on the spot in this country's capital. The commander was
the occupant of a comfortable room in one of Oslo's best
hotels on April 9. He had registered there a few days before
wearing civilian clothes, his uniform in a trunk. According
to the hotel register he was a German stocking salesman
on a business trip.

This was just one Trojan horse maneuver. Germans in
civilian clothes had been sent in large numbers to Norway
in previous months, posing as friendly tourists. Actually
they were spies equipped with cameras and binoculars and
well schooled in the art of spotting anything of military
importance to an invader. The German command also made
sure that many of the troops chosen for the invasion had
visited Norway before and knew something of the language.

A good manpower reservoir was available for this. There
were many Germans of fighting age who as youngsters, ail-
ing from starvation diets during World War I, had been
cared for and restored to health by hospitable Norwegian
families. These men would prove just as merciless as any
other soldiers, their attitude devoid of any gratefulness toward their one-time friends.

Oslo, which has a population of some 300,000 persons,
was taken over by some 1500 airborne troops landed at
Fornebu airfield. These were already under effective control
by the time seaborne forces arrived in the capital.

Details of what had happened did not become known to
the outside world until almost a week after the onslaught.
They were contained in the dispatches of veteran American
newsman Leland Stowe of the Chicago *Daily News*. Stowe
was in Oslo when the Germans came. When the German
censors stopped all his reports, he made his way to Sweden
and flashed his news to a startled world from Stockholm
in detailed articles.

"Norway's capital and great seaports were not captured
by armed force," he wrote. "They were seized with unparalleled speed by means of a gigantic conspiracy which

must undoubtedly rank among the most audacious, most perfectly oiled political plots of the past century."

On April 9 the stocking salesman, having duly changed into proper military apparel, marched at the head of the 1500-man German column through the city.

"They [the German troopers] were hard-muscled, stony-faced men," Stowe reported. "They marched with guns on their shoulders, with beautiful precision. Mostly they stared straight ahead, but some could not restrain triumphant smiles toward the onlookers. Several times General von Falkenhorst and the two other officers (walking alongside the commander) returned Nazi salutes from persons in the crowd who must have been German advance agents who had been busy in Oslo for weeks before the crowning moment. From our hotel balcony two Nazis gave the salute."

In mountain fastnesses, in the valleys, along the fjords, in city, town, and villages, from the Arctic zone southward to the North Sea, the flames of underground resistance in this northernmost bastion of future "Fortress Europa" gradually intensified.

There could be no compromise with the Germans and Quisling and his henchmen, including the armed Quisling thugs known as Hirds. Secret resistance networks began coalescing and going into action, naturally very limited at first, almost immediately after the invasion. Before it was all over the Germans and Quislings would have good cause to remember the word "joessing."

As soon as the Germans had arrived, Quisling proclaimed himself Prime Minister of Norway but this so-called government—a shadow one if anything—only lasted till April 15. He had no real influence among Norwegians and loyal government officials, both high and low, gave him the stiff elbow at every opportunity.

This regime was supplanted by a Council of Administration grouping loyal Norwegians of high standing, to ensure the continued functioning of civil affairs and prevent possible chaos. The formation of this council was proposed by Paul Berg, Chief Justice of the Supreme Court. It was endorsed by King Haakon, then in England, to save the country further evils. This body operated until February 1, 1942, when Quisling, whose personal ambition was unquenchable, again became Prime Minister of Norway with German support. He held this post with considerable ineptitude until the end of the war.

Throughout the occupation the real power, as in other countries, lay in the hands of German military and civilian authorities, the latter personified in Norway by the odious Reichskomissar Joseph Terboven.

What the Germans never did find out during the occupation was that the man who was one of the most influential resistance leaders of Norway was none other than Paul Berg, aided in part by other members of the Supreme Court. It was they who made most of the big decisions in regard to the activities of the resistance which gradually developed into two main divisions: Sivorg, embracing civilian activities, such as illegal newspapers and other anti-Nazi propaganda, and Milorg, the armed attack and sabotage grouping. As in other countries, specially trained men, mostly Norwegians, smuggled in by land, sea and air, aided materially in many operations, becoming an integral part of the movement.

THE HOUSE OF SHRIEKS

The Germans sought by all possible means to prevent news of Nazi atrocities from leaking out of occupied lands. Detailed accounts, however, began to reach England and other countries, more and more of them, some of the most important provided by escapees from Nazi prisons or those who managed to flee from occupied territory.

The Norwegian Information Service in New York City, an official organ of the Norwegian government, has in its library a small official booklet entitled *The Gestapo at*

Work in Norway. It contains accounts of persons who had actually been targets of atrocities. They were formally interviewed and their stories thoroughly checked by a prominent Norwegian judge assigned by King Haakon's government to this task. The booklet was published in the early war years in London and elsewhere, its authenticity beyond question.

Just what faced any persons defying or displeasing the Nazis during World War II is vividly portrayed in one of these accounts, probably that of a joessing.

"Even the Quislings look at the curtained windows of the building with an uneasy feeling," the Norwegian told the judge, referring to Victoria Terrasse, *Gestapo* headquarters in Oslo. "If one goes there with a completely clear conscience—to obtain a pass or seek permission to visit a friend or relations in prison—one gets a paralyzing feeling of uneasiness and fear when one goes through the main gates.

"The long rows of SS patrol cars and ambulances which stand outside remind one of the Norwegians who perhaps at that very moment are undergoing treatment from the Gestapo torturers. It may happen that while you stand and wait to get a pass to go on holiday, you hear desperate, heart-rending cries from prisoners on the floor above. You perhaps look fearfully and questioningly at the German office girl. She merely shrugs her shoulders in a non-committal manner and mumbles something about Norwegian idiots.

"You remember what you have heard about prisoners who have jumped from the windows on the fourth floor; they preferred death to inhuman tortures.

"Victoria Terrasse is not a prison, but prisoners are brought there to be interrogated according to the best German principles. These German torturers probably received their training at some German university where the main course has been instruction in methods of physical and mental torture. Many times a day one hears the commands of the Gestapo shouted to prisoners who are being driven up

Karl Johan Street from No. 19 Moellergaten (the chief Oslo prison) to Victoria Terrasse for interrogation.

"I have myself been driven as a prisoner at great speed up Oslo's main street. I was taken from my home early in the morning and they gave me five minutes in which to dress while German soldiers stood in my bedroom.

"I was brutally pushed into the waiting car and then driven at full speed to Victoria Terrasse. I cannot remember very well what I felt during that few minutes' ride. I was certainly paralyzed with fear because I remember I was unsteady on my feet when I was pushed through the main entrance to the building and I found it difficult to climb the narrow steps into the guardroom.

"I probably wondered what I would feel like when I came back down those steps. In the guardroom there were two dogs,* one at each door. It is funny how well I remember the details in this waiting-room to hell. On one wall there was a large portrait of Hitler and on another, a poster. Behind the desk was the German SS Officer, Worthmann, a typical Prussian, brutal and terrifying.

"I was pushed over to the desk and Worthmann cried '*Achtung!*' (attention) and all the German guards clicked their heels together. The whole room seemed to tremble.

" 'Now you are going to confess, you pro-English swine.' These were the first words flung at me. Then the interrogation began. These interrogations can last up to fifteen hours at a time. Four Germans relieve each other at fixed intervals. The accused must stand throughout the interrogation, while the Germans continually move about. They appear restless and nervous. This is done in order to make the prisoner nervous. You are to be broken by screams, shouted orders and sharp, blinding light. They focus a strong beam of light on you. They use the most terrifying threats. They tempt you with large sums of money, good positions, mild sentences—if you will only confess.

* Probably German shepherd dogs.

"If after a long period of interrogation they have not got anything out of the prisoner, he is put either into a dark cell or a hot cell. The dark cell is in the cellar, a little cold room equipped only with a small wooden stool. At certain intervals two German soldiers enter. One of them holds the prisoner while the other one directs a strong light on the face of the victim. All the time they scream that you must confess. But if you are strong you remain there for days and you forget the time. But by degrees you are collapsing.

"The hot cell is a little cupboard built into the wall and there is just enough room for one man. Rings are put under your arms to hold you up when you faint. In the ceiling there is a little ventilation hole while the heat pours in through the floor of the cupboard. After a while you will lose consciousness and when you are let out, after hours which seem like days, you may be broken down, weak and ill. If you are a Norwegian you will stand up to the strain of this cell all the same.

"There are other rooms in this unpleasant building where the treatment is even more devilish. These torture rooms are on the third and fourth floors. They are large, dark rooms where no daylight can enter. The walls are covered with soundproof material, and in the ceiling there are large lamps which can be regulated. In a corner there is a chair much like a dentist's chair. On one wall there is a portrait of Hitler, on the opposite wall one of Himmler. The room is in half-darkness.

"One can see the guards in the background like shadows, immovable, at attention. The only one who speaks is one of the torturers. It may be either Westerberger, Gussler, Bernhard, or Fehmer (all *Gestapo* officers). He goes constantly backwards and forwards, to and fro, and in his hand is either a stick or a revolver.

"The man I met there was Westerberger. He seemed melancholy, almost despairing, and talked a lot about 'the homeland' and the music of Schubert. Suddenly he attacked me with full fury. Before I had even said a single word he hit and kicked me until I lost consciousness. When I regained consciousness the light in the ceiling was switched on and its glaring beams poured into my eyes. Then it began all over again. The torturers alternately struck out at me or screamed for a confession.

"If the walls of Victoria Terrasse could speak they would tell of hundreds of Norwegians who have been tortured and plagued, of tears and blood, of strong young Norwegians who came in well and healthy and who were carried out either as dead men or physical wrecks. But these walls can also speak of courage and endurance, of love of the homeland and belief that one day the good will triumph, of the hopes which sustained them even under the worst torture."

THE GREAT SKI RAID
AND OTHER EPISODES

Snaking swiftly down a snow-covered mountain flank in the Hardanger Vidda, the nine Norwegian skiers headed for the forbidding chasm near Rjukan on a bitterly cold night of late February 1944.

In the knapsacks of some of the men were plastic explosives. All were armed with knives and Sten guns or revolvers. SOE-trained commandos, they were crack shots, adept in the silent kill and sabotage.

As they silently descended the steep hill, plumes of snow eddying in their wake, they could vaguely see their target for that night: a big building on the other side of the gorge in their path.

The big building was an industrial plant controlled by the Germans. It was not just another plant manufacturing arms or routine military material. Its output was very special. The scientific name for it was heavy water.

Located in the central part of southern Norway, the Hardanger Vidda is one of the largest, loneliest, and wildest mountain areas in northern Europe. Here rise tier on tier

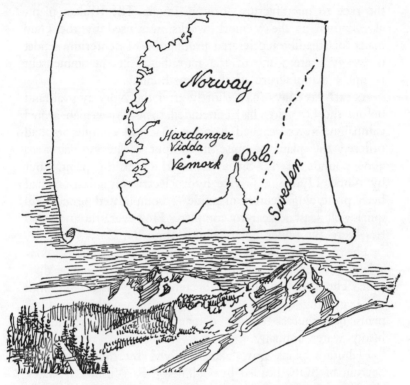

of rugged mountains, mostly barren, soaring skyward to heights ranging from 3300 to 4200 feet above sea level. Only during short summer spells does grass or moss grow among the rocks and snow. Raging snowstorms and bitter winds lash the mountain flanks and valleys of the Hardanger Vidda during many weeks of the year. It is the abode of wild animals, including large herds of reindeer, its human population small. Only the most daring and hardy skiers or mountaineers tackle this terrain in wintertime.

The plant is in the heart of this zone, near Rjukan, perched on a high, inaccessible spur like some medieval castle. Today it manufactures fertilizer. During World War II, however, it had a far more sinister significance. Located some seventy miles due west of Oslo, the plant was a vital component of German endeavors to outstrip the Allies in the race to manufacture an atom bomb. The Rjukan plant, also known as the Vemork works, was used by the Germans for steadily accelerated production of deuterium oxide, or heavy water, one of the ingredients in the immensely complex manufacture of the atom bomb.

As early as May, 1940, shortly after the Norway grab and before the Hitlerites had concluded their Norwegian armed campaign, news reached London that the conquerors had ordered the plant to raise its output of heavy water to 3000 pounds yearly. Since before the war the plant, built by Norsk Hydro, a private hydroelectric organization, had been producing deuterium oxide—a complicated process requiring at least a year to complete. However, these quantities were far under 3000 pounds annually.

The news immediately made the plant a point of considerable interest to the British, notably the espionage division. The problem did not become really disturbing until the beginning of 1942, when it was learned that the Germans had increased their demands to 10,000 pounds of heavy water annually.

Elaborate plans now were evolved by the Norwegian Section of SOE, headed by Colonel J. S. Wilson, to knock the plant out of commission and thus deal a serious blow to any German plans to make an atom bomb ahead of the Allies. The best method, it was decided, would be a commando-type raid by Norwegians trained in Britain by SOE and parachuted into the forbidding area.

Fortunately, Professor Leif Tronstad, one of the greatest experts on Norwegian industry, was in London. This expert knew in detail all the complicated equipment used in the production of heavy water and the layout of the Rjukan plant as well.

A complex parachute drop operation was evolved, whose key men would eventually consist of eleven Norwegian commandos, their sole target the heavy water plant. All would be equipped with skis and be skillful in their use, something which is virtually second nature to all Norwegians.

Before leaving for Norway each man would be a thoroughly trained commando, each familiar with the terrain, weather conditions, and the plant complex itself, which had been carefully re-created in model form in London.

Assigned to a preliminary scouting expedition, Norwegian commando Einar Skinnarland was dropped in the Hardanger Vidda on March 28, 1942, along with containers bearing various equipment including tents, food concentrates, skis, plastic explosives, ammunition and light wireless equipment. Einar landed without injury in the very difficult terrain and reconnoitered the area during the late spring and summer months, sending valuable wireless reports to London.

On October 19, 1942, four other Norwegian commandos were dropped in the zone and after some difficulties joined up with Skinnarland, bringing in more supplies. To bolster the operation, Britain attempted its first glider operation of the war the following month, on November 19, 1942, with British commandos trained in mountain warfare.

This ended in tragedy.

One glider seeking to land in appalling weather conditions, marked by a blizzard, crashed into a mountain, killing the two pilots, the commander of the detachment and seven of his men outright. Others were seriously injured and caught by the Germans. The injured were taken to Stavanger hospital, where they were poisoned and their bodies, weighted with stones, thrown into the sea. Five uninjured men were taken to Grini prison and at dawn on January 18, 1943, were shot as spies.

Another glider and its towing aircraft were unable to find the Rjukan area due to the stormy conditions and turned homeward. The air was intensely cold, however, and enroute the tow rope became so heavily iced that it snapped and the glider made a crash landing near Helleland in the Hardanger Vidda zone. Three of its occupants were killed in landing and the remainder captured and taken to a German camp at Egersund in southern Norway. They were executed a few hours later, accused of being spies.

All the men were in uniform but a fateful oversight gave the Germans the excuse they needed for such brutal action. Civilian clothes had been stowed in the gliders for eventual use by the commandos.

Early in 1943, in the first part of February, six other Norwegians, led by the veteran, Captain Knut Haukelid, took off from Britain for the snow-blanketed Hardanger Vidda. The drop was successful although all the men narrowly missed death and encountered considerable difficulty in rounding up their supply containers. In a few days the men of this group, known as Gunnerside, joined up with Einar Skinnarland and the four men who had dropped together in October, known as the Grouse party.

On Thursday, February 25, Haukelid and eight of the men, armed with fast-firing hand weapons and heavy packs containing food and explosives, snapped on their ski bindings, and left their tent headquarters deep in the mountains. Einar Skinnarland and Knut Haugland were left behind since they were wireless operators and were not essential to the raiding party.

The raiders had carefully estimated their traveling time. By Saturday, February 27, they would be in a good jumping-off position near the Rjukan works. They would strike at the plant on Sunday, February 28.

"The Germans no doubt considered that Vemork was so well protected by nature that it would be difficult for attackers to reach it," Knut Haukelid reported later. "The works lie like an eagle's eyrie high up on the mountainside. In front the way is completely barred by a deep and sheer ravine, cut by the Maan River in its thousand years' journey to the sea. Its waters with unwearying toil have made a perpendicular-sided crack in the bottom of the valley. Across this crack, the Germans thought no one could make his way."

So deep is the gorge that sunlight seldom reaches the bottom area. A narrow suspension bridge about 75 feet long crossed the ravine at one point—and still does—and this was kept under constant guard.

From the bridge a steep, narrow path led up to the factory. At the back of the buildings the hill was very steep, and was partly covered with rough ice. The only way down the hill was a long flight of steps beside a pipeline. The area around the pipeline and around the fence enclosing the works was mined. Machine guns had been posted at various vital points and strong searchlights were ready to bolster defense against any night attack.

There was one very encouraging factor for the commandos. Reconnaissance in previous weeks had ascertained that only fifteen armed guards protected the plant, a very low number in view of its importance.

The commandos struck through the ravine. Half an hour before midnight, Saturday, they assembled in a deserted hut some six hundred yards from the plant, undetected in the darkness. Their skis had been hidden in the snow when they had reached the vicinity of the plant.

Shortly after midnight, the commandos succeeded in piercing the protective fence around the plant by using a wirecutter to break a chain holding one of the gates shut. Two of the men were detailed to enter the building and set explosives in designated spots while the others covered them outside. The two men first tried to get through one of the doors on the ground floor but this had to be abandoned. Eventually they crawled in through a cable intake and moved along pipes under the floor and reached a door leading to the room containing the main heavy water installations. The door was opened and the night watchman was suddenly confronted by two men in British uniforms with Norwegian insignia on the shoulders.

The barrel of a revolver held by one of the Norwegians kept him quiet while the other commando set the explosives. Shortly before the fuses were ignited and set for an explosion in two minutes time, the Norwegians told the watchman to run for it, which he did, vanishing through one of the doors in the room.

The commandos then made a hurried exit through

another door and rejoined their comrades outside. Thus far German guards in a wooden hut just outside the plant had not been aroused. Haukelid and several other men of his party had the hut zeroed in with tommy guns.

"At last there was an explosion, but an astonishingly small, insignificant one," Haukelid recalled. "Was this what we had come over a thousand miles to do? Certainly the windows were broken and a glimmer of light spread out into the night, but it was not particularly impressive."

The Germans apparently were not alerted by the reverberation. It was several minutes before they reacted.

A single German came out of the hut, went over and felt the door leading to the electric-light plant. It was locked and he went in again. But a moment later he reappeared with a flashlight in his hand. He walked toward Haukelid and another Norwegian named Jens Paulsson standing in readiness in deep shadow and flicked the light along the ground.

Jens put his finger on the trigger.

"Shall I fire?" he asked.

"No, he doesn't know what has happened. Leave him be as long as possible," Haukelid said, knowing that their task was to blow things up, not rub out one German more or less.

The man directed his beam on the ground behind them, and once more Jens raised his weapon. But the German turned and went in again.

Shortly before 1:00 A.M. all nine commandos had reassembled and scrambled down the ravine after picking up their skis, which would be used again as soon as convenient.

When they reached the bottom of the valley they heard the alarm sirens sound off, the German signal for a general alert in the Rjukan area. High up on the crest where the plant was located they could see the flash of searchlights and the beams of flashlights as the Germans, obviously aware that an armed attack had taken place, sought to locate the culprits.

The Norwegians were too elusive however. Late on Sunday they reached a small hut on the shores of Lake Langesjaa. After a day's rest they moved deeper into the mountains and finally contacted the two wireless operators.

A jubilant wireless message was sent to London station: HIGH-CONCENTRATION INSTALLATION AT VEMORK COMPLETELY DESTROYED ON NIGHT OF 27–28 STOP GUNNERSIDE HAS GONE TO SWEDEN STOP GREETINGS.

It had been decided that the whole party should now disperse, some to Sweden, some to southern Norway. Haukelid and Arne Kjelstrup, one of the men of Grouse, remained in the mountain area during part of the spring of 1943 and then became active in resistance work elsewhere in southern Norway.

The explosion at Vemork had created an uproar among the Nazis. Late Sunday morning German reinforcements rushed to the scene, followed by no less a person then Reichscomissar Terboven and the stocking salesman von Falkenhorst. Terboven wanted immediately to shoot ten hostages who had been arrested but he was countermanded by von Falkenhorst.

The fifteen guards came in for some unpleasant moments facing von Falkenhorst. The guards were wearing great sheepskin coats with collars turned up and caps pulled low over their eyes as protection against the cold.

"You look like a lot of Father Christmasses!" he roared. "You can't see or hear saboteurs with all those clothes on! Besides, you're up against the most dangerous men the enemy has . . ."

Von Falkenhorst then ordered a sweeping search of the Hardanger Vidda area by German troops, many of them on skis, but it all led to nothing.

The attack on the plant, however, had not been a telling one, as Haukelid and his friends in Norway and London learned by early summer, 1943. After four months of fever-ish work the Germans had succeeded in getting the plant into full production again and were planning to increase its output.

In the fall the Allies in London decided to strike at the plant from the air. Two attacks were made by both British and American planes but the target, surrounded by high mountains, was an elusive pinpoint and the raids were only partially successful. The bombs did not destroy any great amount of heavy water but they did cause the Germans to stop production temporarily.

By the winter of 1943, Haukelid, Einar Skinnarland, Rolf Sorlie, a man from the Rjukan area, and several other companions were again in the Hardanger Vidda.

On January 29, 1944, London radioed:

IT IS REPORTED THAT THE HEAVY WATER APPARATUS AT VEMORK IS TO BE DISMANTLED AND TRANSPORTED TO GERMANY STOP CAN YOU GET THIS CONFIRMED? STOP CAN THIS TRANSPORT BE PREVENTED?

Haukelid, after considerable espionage on Rjukan and its vicinity, informed London that he believed it could be done in spite of sweeping German security measures.

He learned that the Germans intended to remove the heavy water in barrels along with vital machinery via train to Lake Tinnsjo, about twenty miles east of Rjukan. There the entire shipment would be placed on a ferry boat and transported to the southern end of the lake.

Any attack against the plant itself was now out of the question, as well as any attempt against the train, which all knew would be heavily guarded. The Norwegians determined somehow to place explosives on the ferry before the transshipment from the train had been made at the small lakeshore village of Mel. Learning that the train from Rjukan would reach Mel shortly before 10:00 A.M., Sunday, February 20, and that the ferry would leave with its valuable cargo shortly after 10:00 A.M., the Norwegians decided to strike boldly about midnight on the night of February 19–20.

Shortly after midnight Saturday, February 19, Haukelid, Rolf, and another man from Rjukan who had volunteered to help, crept past the Mel station and headed for the ferry. All carried Sten guns, revolvers, and hand grenades in addition to bags of explosives. They planned to pretend to Norwegian crew members aboard that they had to escape from the Rjukan area and wanted to hide aboard the ferry and head south.

The bitterly cold night set everything creaking and crackling; the ice on the road snapped sharply as they went over it. When they came out on the bridge by the ferry station, it seemed as if there was as much noise as if a whole company was on the march.

About three-quarters of a mile distant was an automobile which had been used to transport Haukelid, Rolf, the Rjukan man, and two other Norwegians, including a driver, to the vicinity of the ferry boat. The driver was in the car as the men closed in on the ferry, instructed to keep his motor running for instant flight and to take off immediately if he heard any shots.

Haukelid, Rolf, and their Rjukan friend succeeded in quietly boarding the ferry, while one of the band kept them covered from a vantage point on the dock.

The raiders went below and found a hatchway to the bilge. Before they got the hatch open they heard steps, and took cover behind a nearby table and chairs. The ferry watchman was standing in the doorway. He must have left the game of poker which the trio had ascertained was underway in the crew's quarters after hearing some suspicious noise. Haukelid told him that he and Rolf were seeking to escape the Germans.

The watchman told them that he and other crew members on several previous occasions had helped Norwegians escape aboard the ferry and that he was ready to help them. The hatchway was opened and Knut and Rolf disappeared below. In the meantime, the Rjukan man kept the ferryman engaged in a long chat above, because it was imperative that what was really afoot should not be known.

Working hastily in a cramped area covered by foot-deep bilge water, Knut and Rolf completed the somewhat complex rigging of their explosive charge by flashlight. They placed it forward in the ferry in a concealed spot so that when it exploded and water poured into the ship, its bow would go down first. They had estimated that the charge would blow a hole about eleven square feet in the ship's side. Two alarm clocks would touch off the explosion. The blasts were scheduled for 10:45 A.M. Sunday, when the ferry would be over the deepest part of the lake, one of the deepest in Norway.

Everything ready, Rolf and Knut returned to the watchman still talking with the Rjukan man. While the work had been going on below he had told the watchman that they would have to return to Rjukan hurriedly to fetch some things they had forgotten, but would be back in the morning and in their hiding place in good time before the ship's departure.

Then the three raiders left the ferry, picked up their cover, and headed for the car, which sped off in the night. All men were sorrowful over one factor—there would be loyal Norwegian crewmen aboard the ferry on the morrow. To have warned them of what was impending was too dangerous. They would have to be sacrificed.

The party then dispersed, Haukelid heading for Oslo which he reached late on Monday. All he wanted to know was in the newspapers that evening, an event which even the controlled German newspapers revealed because they knew it could not be kept secret very long.

The headline on every front page was RAILWAY FERRY *HYDRO* SUNK IN THE TINNSJO.

The stories added that the ferry had sunk in a few minutes and was lying in deep water. Fourteen Norwegians and four German guards had gone down with her. Whether other

German guards were aboard and possibly had succeeded in getting to shore was never revealed. Success was complete.

In view of its scientific implications and the difficult terrain, the action against the heavy water plant was labeled by high Allied authorities as the most significant sabotage operation of modern war.

Malice toward some

As was to be expected, in the midst of the Nazi oppression humorous incidents—at least amusing to the oppressed—occurred and were widely retold in Norway.

The failure of the Germans to invade England was the cause of numerous such episodes. There was one Norwegian story about an old woman who used to sit on the edge of a pier during the evening hours just before curfew. One evening an automobile packed with four or five drunken German soldiers and noncoms came careening down the peer, spun out of control a few yards away from her, and plunged into the murky water, sinking like a stone. There were no survivors.

In short order Quisling police, having witnessed the accident from a distance, came running down the pier. After looking at the oily water, they turned angrily on the old woman and shouted:

"You, why didn't you warn them, you saw them coming?"

"Oh," the woman replied her face expressionless, "I thought they were going to England."

On another occasion a German corporal accosted a pretty Norwegian girl clerk in a big department store with a "Heil Hitler!" and the question, "Where is the hosiery division?"

Quickly the girl replied, "God Save the King, second floor."

In the summer of 1940 boys in a Norwegian town saw a German soldier goose-stepping across a drill field blowing on a Scottish bag-pipe, followed by laughing comrades singing the popular German ditty *Wir fahren gegen England* (We are sailing against England).

To a question from one of the boys, a German soldier who spoke some Norwegian said that they were learning how to play the bagpipe in preparation for Nazi occupation of Scotland.

As the weeks passed and the British bastion held firm, the Germans saw many boys pantomiming bagpipe playing until they deemed it advisable to take to their heels.

THE DOOMED SHIPS

Moment of truth

A surprise visit by six burly, uniformed thugs of Quisling's secret police detained Max Manus—but not for long—in his small apartment on the second story of 4 Vidarsgate, Oslo, on Sunday, January 16, 1941.

Young Manus, a slim blond Norwegian of twenty-seven, had headed for his apartment after another full day's work in the capital—underground activity. Max already was a veteran at this type of thing, having been active in the capital and elsewhere for about nine months. He was one of the promising members of a growing resistance movement whose activities included the regular publication of an illegal newspaper entitled *Vi Vil Oss et Land* (*We Want a Free Country*).

On that fateful Sunday he had labored on various articles for the next issue with another young Norwegian in a small shack in a little-frequented street of the city.

At the end of the day he bade farewell to his friend, stuffed various texts and messages in a rucksack, slipped it on his back, mounted a rather battered bicycle and pedaled toward 4 Vidarsgate. Plans for an assassination were uppermost in his mind. His group had received secret instructions from London to liquidate an important Quisling government official named Hagelin. Max had been nominated to mastermind this coup.

Max had not adopted an assumed name up to this time. As

far as the Germans were concerned he was just another clerk in a small office. He had never been arrested or questioned by the German or Quisling police, something which they would have cause to regret in the future. On January 16, Max, who would have many faces and names in the years to come, would have good cause to regret something essential—a momentary lapse in his usual high-pitched sixth sense of danger.

Dismounting from his bicycle and leaving it in the main hallway of 4 Vidarsgate, Max ascended the stairs three at a time.

"I noticed nothing special and took out my key to let myself into the apartment," he recalled in memoirs written after the war. "I had a moment's debate with myself whether I should leave the rucksack outside; then I dismissed this idea. At that moment I was plagued by anxiety that comes with fatigue and letdown after many hours of concentrated work."

Not a sound came from the apartment. He inserted the key in the lock, turned it and pushed open the door. He had just crossed the threshold when six men converged on him shouting "*Staatspolitiet!*"

"These, of course, were members of the Quisling Gestapo," Max wrote, adding somewhat humorously, "you know, there is not much one can do in a situation like that. In a book of adventures the hero would have beaten down the first with his bare fists, kicked the second, snatched a gun from the third, shot the fourth and then held up the remaining two. That's how things happen in the movies. I couldn't have managed one sixth of this program. All I did was to smile fatuously and reply even more fatuously: 'Good evening. How are you?'"

This had no soothing effect on the policemen who had been tipped off by a pro-Nazi informant that Max was a very active resistance man.

"They jumped at me then. When they had finished going over me I stood rather lonely and deserted, stripped of the rucksack and its dangerous contents with all my pockets turned inside out."

With visions of Victoria Terrasse before his eyes, Max desperately thought of various ways of getting away. He knew many names. He was not armed and had no cyanide pill—those would be provided only in later months. There were some fifty pounds of dynamite cached in the flat's small bedroom.

He asked somewhat quaveringly whether he could go into the bedroom to get an aspirin. A blunt "no" was the answer from a hulking policeman who seemed to be in command. The man already was opening the rucksack.

"When this didn't work I tried another plan," Max recalled. "I put up my hand with a gesture every schoolboy uses and asked permission to go to the toilet."

Meeting with another blunt refusal, he insisted that he had to go, that he was in a state of shock. The police agreed but he went to the toilet under escort of two policemen, automatics in hand. This finished any hopes Max may have had of slipping out through the back door and down the stairs.

Led back into the living room he saw that the police leader was scanning the material he had taken out of the rucksack. There was a gleam of triumph on his face.

The thought of torture and execution, Max remembered, was like a "bayonet pricking me in the rear."

He swiftly estimated the distance between himself and the window. Then with a somewhat boastful gesture and a loud "look over there at those" he pointed to some medals hanging on a wall. They were medals he had received while fighting as a volunteer with the Finns in their war against Russia, which had ended in March of the previous year.

The gesture and the words had their effect. The eyes of all six policemen swung away from Max toward the wall.

In that split second, facing his own agonizing moment of truth, the young Norwegian bounded toward the window and dove head first through blackout paper and heavy glass. Two stories below was a concrete sidewalk.

The policemen dashed to the window, saw the crumpled form below, and headed on the double for the stairs.

The fishing rod

The next thing Max remembered between spells of unconsciousness was being wheeled along a hospital corridor and placed in a bed. It was Ullevaal Hospital. The police had rushed him there in a car, not prompted by any kindly thoughts, merely so that he would remain alive long enough to be given a grueling interrogation mixed with torture.

X-rays revealed that he had suffered a broken shoulder, back damage, and head concussion. He was placed in a single occupancy room, two of the policemen remaining with him throughout the night.

The next morning, feeling somewhat better after a restful night under sedation, Max succeeded in conveying to the very pretty nurse who was caring for him that he was an important personage in the resistance. This was done while the two guards were momentarily outside the room, conversing in the hall. The nurse assured him that he would be helped and that his doctor could be fully trusted.

The joessing machinery in the hospital started working smoothly. The nurse posted a placard on the door of the room stating ADMISSION STRICTLY FORBIDDEN and told the Quisling guards they would have to get out. The guards protested but the nurse was insistent, stating that the doctor had decided Max was as good as dead. The guards agreed but warned that a permanent watch would be maintained in the hall outside, guards relieving each other at regular intervals.

When the doctor made his rounds later that day he informed Max that he was not too seriously hurt and that his recovery was certain.

Endowed with a strong constitution, Max began recovering satisfactorily but the illusion that he was doomed was skillfully maintained. He was never permitted to leave the bed and when the guards peered in he acted as if he were unconscious.

Bleak as the prospects of escape were, Max was not a man who gave up readily. He had brushed with danger in his middle teens doing various kinds of work in remote areas of South America and had been hardened in combat in some stiff winter fighting between the Finns and the Russians.

Lying in bed, his thoughts centered on the window of his room, which was on the second floor, overlooking a plot of bare ground. This window had been covered with wood as a protection against air attacks. Near the top of the wooden shield was a hatch which was opened every day to let air in. Max came to the conclusion that if the occasion arose he could squeeze through that hatch.

Then Max and the nurse, with the full knowledge of the doctor and nurse friends of hers, evolved a shrewd escape plan. Max arranged a meeting outside the hospital between his nurse and one of his most trusted companions, a teen-ager named Per Jacobsen. In accordance with a message smuggled to him previously, Jacobsen had obtained a stout segmented fishing rod and gave this to the nurse, along with a length of fine, strong fishing line.

The nurse hid this collapsible rod under long full skirts and secreted it in the patient's room, walking right past the two guards with this equipment on her person.

The escape plan was a rather simple one but would need excellent timing and luck. Per Jacobsen and another man at a designated time would drive up in a car to the vicinity of the wing containing Manus' room and park it immediately after the night watchman had passed by that point. Then Jacobsen would cut a hole in the fence surrounding the hospital grounds and sneak up just below the patient's window. Max would at the same time stick the fishing pole through the hatch and unreel the weighted line. The man below would attach a long stout rope to the line and Max would haul it up through the hatch. Once this was done the heavy rope would be fastened securely to a sturdy heating pipe in the room and Max would squeeze through the hatch and slide down to Jacobsen.

The plan could not be carried out immediately. Max would have to be in good ambulatory condition before anything could be done. January merged into February before any additional concrete steps were taken. During this period the doctor and nurses repeatedly had to stall off the police who were becoming increasingly curious regarding the delay in releasing the supposedly dying man from the hospital.

By February 10 Max's condition was deemed sufficiently good for the flight. A time was set for 3:00 A.M. the following morning. It was doomed to disappointment. Max succeeded in unreeling the weighted fishing line to the ground but there was no answering tug. After a long wait he had to pull it in again. By noon the nurse had learned what had gone wrong—Jacobsen had not been able to obtain a car which had been promised him for this occasion.

A new time was set—3:00 A.M., February 12. Shortly before that hour the nurse entered his room past the half-slumbering guards in the hall and stopped alongside the patient's bed.

"She gave me a warning look to be silent and to move stealthily. Again I put the fishing rod outside the window and let the line dangle. At once I felt an answering tug. A second tug on the line and I began reeling in faster and faster. Presently the end of a heavy rope came through the hatch. I caught it and the nurse and I made it fast. . . ."

Max hardly appeared to be a man clothed for a getaway on a cold, wintry early morning. He was wearing a long hospital nightgown and a pair of light slippers on his feet, nothing else.

Both making as little noise as possible, the nurse helped him onto the broad window sill. Before starting to clamber through the hatch he did something both had agreed upon to forestall *Gestapo* suspicions that the nurse was an accessory to his escape.

He bent down and kissed her and then sent her reeling to the floor with a left to the jaw.

"I slithered through the hatch, like a lizard getting under a stone, twisted my feet around the rope and held on to it with my left hand—my right arm was still of little use. I slid down it slowly, while the boys held the rope aslant from the wall, my hospital nightshirt flapping around my bare knees and my bare backside sticking out into the icy cold."

The three sprinted to the garden wall, crept through the hole, and tumbled into the waiting automobile. A nurse in the car immediately gave Max an injection to counteract his extreme fatigue. As the car swung away he was helped into warm clothing.

"We had hardly started and were driving along Kirkevien when we heard police cars come tearing up to Ullevaal Hospital, their sirens shrieking," Max wrote. "My flight had been discovered and an alarm already had been turned in."

Suspicious of noises they had heard, the guards had rushed into the room a few minutes after Max had left. The pretty nurse was lying on the floor, feigning semi-consciousness her jaw red from the blow. The fishing rod was already hidden in the room. She had untied the rope when Max reached the ground. That he took with him. She reiterated stubbornly that she knew nothing of how the patient had escaped since he had suddenly hit her into unconsciousness when she entered the room that night.

Max was deposited at a small village about thirty miles from Oslo. Here he was given a powerful automatic and skis. He reached a hut in a lonely stretch of forest where the resistance had planned in advance to hide him. Although still quite weak, Max stayed alone in the hut for twelve days. Resistance comrades and a nurse from a nearby village dropped in at various intervals, bringing him extra food and medicine.

"My photograph and a description of me were posted everywhere in the country. Thank God it was not a good photograph but just the same this made it necessary that I alter my appearance as much as possible. My friends dyed my hair and eyebrows."

At the end of February it was decided that Max was ready to escape to Sweden. He had replaced his hospital pallor with a sun tan acquired in strolls in the forest. Cotton packed next to his teeth markedly altered his facial contours.

Accompanied by a noted skier named Andreas Aubert, Max left the Oslo area by train, both posing as men on a skiing jaunt. Max had false papers. Reaching the Swedish border after some harrowing escapes from German questioning, Andreas headed back. Max in a few days reached Stockholm and the Norwegian Legation there.*

In Stockholm Max was informed that he had been appointed an infantry lieutenant in the Norwegian armed units being trained under the aegis of the Royal Norwegian Government-in-Exile and the British. He was under orders to proceed first to Canada and Nova Scotia and later to England for training.

In Stockholm Max met Gregers Gram, his junior by two years. Gregers had actually worked on the same illegal newspaper as Max, but such were the underground precautions against too many contacts among resistants that they had never seen each other. They took an immediate liking to each other—a friendship which would prove significant in the future.

Max could not stay in Stockholm very long as evidence piled up that the Svestapo (Swedish criminal police), prodded by the German *Gestapo*, were out to catch him. With the necessary papers and funds provided by the le-

---

* Max's mother, who was of Danish origin, and his Norwegian father were in Norway during the occupation. They had been amicably separated when Max was nine years old and lived in different areas. Max's three sisters were with his mother. Although his father was questioned several times the Germans did not take any drastic action against these members of the family.

gation, he sped to Helsinki, Finland, in a passenger plane filled with Germans. Gregers remained behind but would join Max later in England. Max learned from him eventually that Svestapo police had swept into his hotel to arrest him at the very moment the Helsinki-bound plane took off.

From Helsinki Max made his way to Leningrad, to Odessa, Russia, and then to Istanbul, Turkey. From Istanbul he and a number of other Norwegians reached England by ship after training stopovers in Nova Scotia and Canada. He arrived in England late in December 1941, about ten months since his departure from 4 Vidarsgate.

Perilous jump

Parachutes billowing overhead, two men in white coveralls swung earthward on March 12, 1943 and alighted in the Lake Oyeren zone near Oslo. The big American Douglas bomber from which they had dropped along with parachute-borne containers, headed for Oslo to drop some leaflets and then droned back to England through the starry night.

The two men were Max Manus and Gregers Gram. The drop was a troublesome one for both of them. It had been planned that they would alight in a soft, swampy area but the timing was off—a not unusual occurrence in such dangerous ventures.

Max barely missed landing on the edge of a terrifying precipice in the hilly, forested region and bumped down on a heap of stones at its base. Fortunately he was not hurt and swiftly released himself from his parachute bindings. After clambering around in the snow he found Gregers in a small hollow nearby. His face was bleeding from minor cuts suffered when his head had bumped against the airplane hatch in jumping out.

It would have been difficult for either friends or enemies to recognize the two parachutists. Experts in England had worked on them. Gregers' blond curly hair had been dyed dark and plastered down with grease. In the mouths of each were rubber pads drastically altering facial contours. Max's hair had been dyed red. Each carried big, horn-rimmed glasses which could be worn to aid their facial disguise.

Under their white coveralls they wore the uniforms of Company Linge, the Norwegian commando force trained for operations in the homeland by SOE and Norwegian officers. The uniforms were British battle dress with the word Norway on the shoulder patch.

Max and Gregers, now respectively lieutenant and sergeant, spent a chill night sleeping side by side in the folds of their parachutes after drinking some rum and eating some cold food. At dawn they hid their parachutes under snow in bushes and started searching for the metal containers. It was not until late in the afternoon, after arduous searching and hauling, that they succeeded in collecting them. At nightfall they pitched a tent in a thick copse of trees and cooked their first hot meal since leaving England.

Both men were in top condition, fully trained commandos. The main purpose of their drop was ship sabotage, their speciality. Their thoughts were on Oslo harbor.

Handsome Gregers had arrived in England early in 1942, also via the Near East, and the friendship which started earlier between Max and him deepened. For months they had undergone rigorous training in England and Scotland, including survival tests on ski trips in the Scottish mountains in terrain somewhat similar to that of Norway.

In addition to physical and arms training "you learned all about secret codes and the use of invisible ink, how to forge papers and how to camouflage those which could not be forged," Max recalled. "There were also courses in lying quickly and smoothly."

During this period both became deeply interested in ship sabotage with limpets, a type of magnetic plastic explosive which could be fastened to the hulls of ships, the explosion controlled by a timing device.

Virtually nothing had been overlooked in equipping them for this raid. Their feet were encased in big boots with heavy rubber innersoles, worn on top of ski boots. Thick rubber plates protected their spines when they jumped and their helmets were of heavy raw rubber, which came down to their necks. Supplies in their pockets included first-aid kits, a twenty-four-hour ration package, morphine, Benzedrine tablets to keep them awake if necessary, and knockout pills. The latter were intended for use against the enemy if the occasion should arise. Dropped in a glass of beer, they would be effective for twenty-four hours. In addition, each carried false identity papers and the usual final solution—cyanide pills.

In the containers were two pairs of skis and poles, a Bren gun, a tommy gun, two rifles, extra ammunition, a tent, civilian clothing of the type then prevalent in Norway, two primus stoves, medicines, and various kinds of food rations. As additional armament each man carried two automatics, hand grenades, long commando knives, compasses, and maps of the Oslo area.

A large quantity of limpets were carefully stowed in special containers. Each limpet weighed twelve pounds and contained one and three-quarter pounds of plastic explosive. It was stowed in an oblong tin box, flat on that side designed to be placed against a ship's hull. This box was about ten inches long and four inches broad, equipped with magnets intended to hold it in position. Each limpet had a firing pin, which when released would drop down on a detonator and set off the charge.

"The firing pin is held back by a spring which, in turn, is kept taut by celluloid," according to a description given by Max. "When the acid in the timing device at the top of the limpet eats through the celluloid, the spring is released, the firing pin drops on the detonator cap and the plastic is exploded."

Immediately after landing Max came down with a raging fever complicated by pneumonia. Cared for by Gregers with the aid of pills with which they had been supplied, Max recovered in three days. A few days thereafter it was decided that Gregers should leave the forest, garbed as a civilian, and proceed to the immediate vicinity of Oslo to contact resistance friends.

After several days had passed, he returned to the tent with a resistance man named Rigert and the three completed hiding the containers at various points, a task which had not been completed due to Max's illness.

The harbor phantoms

Late in March Max and Gregers, both armed with pistols and grenades, headed for a farm near Enebak, owned by a trusted man named Peterssen. Under civilian clothing they wore their uniforms, their bulky appearance not likely to attract undue attention since all civilians wore layers of various warm clothing at this time of year due to the cold.

After a few days in hiding at the farm the two commandos shifted again, this time to the house of another underground man named Henrik Martinsen at Ljan, closer to Oslo harbor. Here they spent their time making further contact with resistance aides in and near Oslo. This was always dangerous. He and Gregers had to take their chances bicycling and walking around in full sight of many Germans. Their disguises were effective, however.

"With glasses on my nose, I looked a lot like the famous American film comedian, Harold Lloyd," Max recalled with a chuckle in later years.

The harbor area was carefully surveyed and the locations of various ships noted. To attack anything, it was evident, would be a very risky business. German patrol boats were on the alert day and night, equipped with searchlights and machine guns while guards patrolled the docks in the vicinity of various freighters operated by the Germans.

After considerable planning, Max and Gregers decided to strike on the night of April 10–11, 1943, which would be moonless.

During that night two canoes, coming from Ljan, sneaked into the harbor zone. In one was Max and a young home front member named Kris Dahlman and in the other Gregers and Henrik Martinsen. Both Gregers and Max were wearing their uniforms, partially screened by sweaters and tweed jackets. In each canoe, which traveled in different directions, were quantities of limpets. Both Gregers and Max were armed with revolvers, grenades, and knives.

Gregers and Martinsen, it had been decided, would go after a 6000-ton Norwegian freighter commandeered by the Germans, another smaller freighter named the *Ortelsburg*, and a coal boat. Max and his companion headed for the 6000-ton S.S. *Tuguela*, a freighter, and another merchantman, the S.S. *Von Knipprode*.

Before heading for the *Tuguela*, Max and Kris stopped off at a small island and planted a limpet on a stone, timed to go off in five or six hours. A short distance away they scattered British cigarettes and nailed a letter to a tree with a knife. The letter contained a defiant message to Admiral Karl Doenitz, commander of the German Navy, implying that secret British forces were operating in the harbor. It was signed "Corporal Brown, submarine commandos." This action was designed to make the Germans believe that any action which occurred was the work of secret British commandos and had nothing to do with Norwegians.

Hugging the shadows, on several occasions narrowly missed by probing searchlight beams of patrol boats, Max and Kris reached the vicinity of the *Tuguela*, coming to a halt in a particularly dark area along a dock. A very ticklish problem now confronted them.

"The crew of the *Tuguela* was working full shift, loading potatoes and other foodstuffs and dismantled barracks destined for the German army. The Germans wanted her to leave as soon as possible and therefore were loading day and night, in spite of blackout regulations. Everything around the ship was brightly lighted . . . the harbor was being combed by searchlights and patrol boats were everywhere."

To reach the *Tuguela* without making a long detour, in paddling close to the docks the canoe would have to cross a brightly lit expanse in full view of anyone on the ship or the nearby wharves.

Both decided to take a gamble rather than lose valuable time.

"Our decision taken, we slid along through the shadows, still close to the quay, until we came to a place with an iron ladder against the wall. I heard steps above, then suddenly all was quiet. I was curious to see what was going on up there. I made a sign to Kris who held the canoe steady, and cautiously I climbed the ladder until my eyes could just look over the top of the quay.

"I was looking straight at a pair of German boots.

"Thank God it was the heels I was looking at. Noiselessly I retreated down the ladder and indicated to Kris that danger was close. Presently the German began to patrol again and I began to breathe. We pulled the canoe along the wall to the end of the quay. Here the water level was illuminated and men were working. There was a lot of noises from winches and cranes . . . between us and the *Tuguela* was a distance from 25–30 meters."

The water here was as brightly lit as in full sunshine.

"I pushed the canoe away from the shadow of the quay. Kris dipped his paddle and we glided out into the spotlight. Several times in my life I have experienced miracles. I saw one that night. I can describe it only by analogy. Imagine a big party in a brightly lighted room. People are standing about, balancing drinks and small sandwiches. All at once an enormous green crocodile slithers across the floor and disappears. What would happen?

"The women would probably scream. But if there were only men at the party, it is more than probable that not one of them would have the moral courage to mention the beast they had seen. Because it was unconventional, irregular, out of order, their defense mechanisms would immediately take warning and persuade them it had no existence. Maybe that is what happened that night in Oslo Harbor."

The canoe got across without being hailed or fired at and got alongside the hull of the *Tuguela.*

". . . As soon as we had rounded her stern and were sheltered by it I put on the first limpet," Max wrote. "Then another ten feet further away; then a third, a fourth. I put them on well below the water level (using a pole with a special attachment to grasp the limpets). It was a wonderful feeling when I brought the pole close to the hull and felt the magnets leap toward the metal plates . . . we moved on to where I guessed the engine room was located and there four more limpets were attached. I wanted the *Tuguela* to go down. It was most wonderful of all when I pulled up the pole after the last one had clung to its prey. The *Tuguela* was doomed . . ."

The limpets were timed to go off at 6:00 A.M., April 11.

Max and Kris decided not to push their luck too far by attacking the *Von Knipprode.* Although the distance was not too great, they would have to cover an illuminated expanse of water some two hundred feet in breadth.

Plying their paddles with utmost vigor they again successfully crossed the lighted zone near the *Tuguela* and headed for a cove near Ljan where the four had agreed to meet. Gregers and Henrik were already there and had succeeded in placing limpets on the *Ortelsburg,* the Norwegian freighter, and the coal barge.

The canoes were hidden for future use and then all four scattered, Gregers and Max heading for the Peterssen farm to await developments.

The explosions began as scheduled at 6:00 A.M. One blast after another ripped the *Ortelsburg* and she sank until only her funnel and top deck area were visible. Twenty-four Germans, it was learned later, were killed and a number severely wounded by the explosions. Ship sirens and sirens ashore started wailing. Patrol boats raced madly toward the sinking *Ortelsburg* to rescue wounded Germans floundering in the water.

Men aboard the *Tuguela* climbed her masts to see what

was happening when all hell broke loose on that ship. The blasts, which wounded many men, some of them mortally, tore gaping holes in her hull. She settled fast in the mud of the harbor, her prow sticking up, her afterdeck submerged, a completely useless wreck. Simultaneously, the coal boat was ripped by explosions and also sank in the harbor.

The limpet on the island also exploded. What the Germans found there convinced them that British commandos had been at work. The news of the blasts caused wild jubilation among Norwegians, who suspected that the joessings had been at work.

Unfortunately, the Norwegian freighter tackled by Gregers and his comrade had been only slightly damaged, apparently due to some defect in the limpets that were used.

Max and Gregers now decided it was time for them to return to England to report on their activities and formulate new plans. Reaching London after a somewhat tense journey via Stockholm they were received by King Haakon and British and Norwegian officers. In reward for their action they both were awarded a high Norwegian decoration, the Military Cross with Sword. Before receiving the decoration both men had been demoted in rank. Max to sergeant and Gregers to corporal! This was due to an odd twist in military regulations whereby they could only hold the higher ranks while on active duty.

The S.S. Monte Rosa

During the late spring and summer weeks of 1943 Max and Gregers pondered new sabotage plans and obtained the aid of experts to improve their limpets.

A new gadget was added to the explosive. This was a release switch. This would make the limpet explode even before the time set should anyone remove it from a hull. Part of this improvement involved the use of salt, which was baked around a little steel arm of the release switch.

Once the limpet was in water the salt would begin to dissolve. This would take exactly one half hour. After the salt had dissolved the steel arm would be set free and the original mechanism of the limpet would work. So long as the limpet was firmly held by magnets to the side of the ship, the steel arm couldn't move, even though the salt was dissolved. If the limpet was removed from the ship after the salt was dissolved, the spring would be released and the explosion would occur immediately. Thus anyone taking the limpet off after the thirty safe minutes would be blown to bits and a big hole blasted in the hull.

In the fall, Gregers and Max, their ranks restored, were again parachuted into the Oslo area, accompanied by two other commandos, Karl Eriksen, a noted Norwegian sportsman, and C. F. Valkendorf, a shipping man in civilian life.

"Harold Lloyd" had undergone new facial alterations. His hair had been dyed black and carefully marcelled. The contours of his face and his nose had been altered giving him a slightly Jewish appearance. A dentist filed his front teeth and covered the stumps with crowns entirely different in shape from his natural teeth. Gregers' make-up remained the same. The facial appearance of the other two men had also been altered with dyes, eyeglasses, and make-up.

The containers which were dropped with the men this time contained some additional material, two diving suits and small inflatable rubber boats. The suits were fitted with a Davis Escape Vest, the apparatus sailors had used to escape from submarines. It consisted of a small bottle of oxygen carried on the chest. A rubber hose connected this with the diver's mouth. The diver breathed in the air through the mouth and his exhaled breath went into a "lung," a bag carried on the chest, where it was chemically cleaned. With this suit a man could stay submerged for half an hour.

The entire situation in Oslo had become much more precarious for the raiders as compared to April. The Germans had intensified their drive against the joessings throughout Norway and harbor protective measures had been markedly tightened.

Max and his companions had set their sights on two main

targets in the harbor, the S.S. *Monte Rosa* and the S.S. *Donau*, both 10,000-tonners. These ships were used regularly to transport men and materials to Denmark and Germany or vice-versa. Very often they carried hapless Norwegians caught in the forced labor draft to Germany, which made these ships special symbols of tyranny to the Norwegians.

On Christmas Eve, 1943, known as Little Christmas in Norway, that country's most important Yuletide celebration time, the commandos decided to undertake their first attack in diving suits against some smaller ships. They did succeed in getting into the water under cover of darkness after hair-raising hide-and-seek adventures with German and Quisling guards. The operation, however, was a total flop.

Max suddenly discovered that his suit was filling with water. He barely managed to return to a dock ladder where Gregers helped him up. A limpet he had around his waist had cut a hole in the suit. Valkendorf and Eriksen, operating elsewhere in the harbor, also narrowly escaped disaster. Caught in a strong current Valkendorf had turned over with his heavy load of limpets. He righted himself but his splashing alerted a guard and he opened fire. Moving with extreme difficulty under the surface they escaped the bullets, but before negotiating a landing, Eriksen had to cut loose his rubber suit and it sank to the bottom.

Following this disappointment, Max went for two months to Stockholm to file reports to London and await new instructions. Here he and a beautiful Norwegian secretary working at the legation fell in love. Both decided to marry as soon as his military assignments ended.

During this period Gregers and other men of the Oslo gang—the name for the Manus group—actively engaged in various daring sabotage and propaganda operations, but shipping for the time being was left alone. Max joined in these activities upon his return.

Neither he nor Gregers had forgotten the ships, however. In the fall of 1944, following the Allied landings in France, the two went after the *Monte Rosa*. With the collusion of various harbor workers they got under a pier where the ship regularly docked. Both were disguised as workmen, overalls over their uniforms, ostensibly engaged in dock repair work.

For more than two days they hid under the pier, their abode a section of a large beam under the pier boards. At night they were plagued by rats seeking to get at their food and air tainted by foul harbor water. The *Monte Rosa* finally did dock at the pier and Gregers, in one of their inflatable rubber boats, succeeded in planting four limpets on the ship's hull. When he returned, Max got into the craft for his turn. The ship, however, was already moving out by this time and Max barely escaped being drawn along in her suction. He was unable to plant any explosives.

The two returned to the apartment of a Mrs. Maeland at 2 Frichs Street where they were living in hiding. Within forty-eight hours they received a wireless message from London declaring HARD LUCK. TRY AGAIN.

To both men this meant that their strike had been a failure, that something had gone wrong, perhaps due to the fact that the *Monte Rosa* had sailed away earlier than they expected. Possibly the Germans had succeeded in neutralizing the limpets in some fashion before they went off.

Actually the limpets attached by Gregers had exploded but only by the time the vessel was anchored in Copenhagen. The blasts had caused considerable damage, involving weeks of repair work. After this had been completed she was transformed into a hospital ship. Max would not know until after the war that their venture was not a complete failure. Gregers would never know it.

Victory and tragedy

Gregers now headed for Sweden and some weeks of rest while Max and his friends continued their Oslo activities. During the fall Max succeeded in having various mechanics build a baby torpedo for use against shipping.

It took weeks of secret testing in isolated coves under cover of darkness before the torpedo could be considered operational. Satisfied it would work, Max and another member of the gang, Roy Nielsen, headed into the harbor at night in one of their canoes with the baby torpedo aboard. Their target was a German destroyer.

"Stealthily we came closer and closer to the destroyer," Max recalled. "Now we could hear the voices of the men aboard her. She was some forty yards away. . . . The canoe lay motionless on the water. I switched on the motor of the torpedo and the sudden noise it made startled me so I nearly dropped it. Now the Germans must discover us. I took aim between the smokestacks. I let go. The torpedo cut across the oily water like a comet cleaving the sky and leaving a glowing wake. We waited for the explosion. We didn't dare paddle, except under cover of the noise.

"*Boom!*

"The canoe lifted out of the water. Immediately Roy started to paddle. I lay down flat in the canoe with the automatics ready to open fire if the searchlight revealed us. But a cloud of steam which belched out of the ship's side must have hidden us completely.

"We made the shore, pulled the canoe up, ran across the island where we had landed to the point where we had hidden a second canoe, in which both of us paddled to the mainland."

The following morning they went to a vantage point from which both could see the destroyer. She was surrounded by smaller boats filled with workmen trying to repair the damage. A few days later she weighed anchor but the underground ascertained later that the blast had put her out of commission for seven months.

After Gregers' return, Max suffered a leg wound when he accidentally discharged a pistol in Mrs. Maeland's apartment. A doctor treated the wound, which was superficial, and said it would heal in a few weeks. Max dutifully stayed in bed for five days. However a big attack on the Norse

Vacuum Oil Company in the Oslo area was imminent and Max decided that wound or no wound he would participate.

Max, Gregers, and other men succeeded in blowing up 120,000 gallons of fuel oil at the plant in a blast which could be heard for miles and made a smooth getaway in an automobile.

Although his wound was healing satisfactorily, it was decided that Max should go to Stockholm again for some further medical attention. Before departing he clapped Gregers on the back and said:

"Goodbye for now, and don't take any foolish risks."

Those were the last words the two companions in arms would exchange.

During his stay in Stockholm Max became increasingly worried over reports of intensifying German police actions against the Norwegian resistance. He was preparing to re-enter Norway on skis at a Swedish frontier guardhouse when his fiancée called from Stockholm telling him he must return to the city immediately. When he arrived there was terrible news. Karl Johan—Gregers' underground name—had been killed, another trusted man named Tallak had been wounded, and several other members of the gang arrested.

Secret messages disclosed that Gregers had met his end on November 10. Things might have turned out otherwise if Max had been there. Time and again, Max had warned his best friend not to trust any Germans. Gregers, however, had stuck to the view that there were Germans, notably intellectuals, who hated the Nazis, loved liberty, and respected the rights of individuals of any nation.

While Max was away, Tallak met two Germans who said they were army deserters and claimed they already had undertaken sabotage operations against Kjeller airfield. Their claim was confirmed after a check-up—they had done some sabotage at that field.

Gregers and Tallak agreed to meet the two men at a café. They were sitting at a table waiting for them to arrive when suddenly five armed men attacked. Gregers and Tallak dropped to their knees and used their overturned table as a barricade. In the shooting which ensued two German attackers were mortally wounded. Gregers was shot through the neck and through the chest. He tried blasting himself and an attacker with a grenade, but he did not have time to loosen the grenade pin before he died. Tallak was hit in the jaw, knocked senseless and taken to a hospital. Then he was transferred to a prison and put to the torture. Tallak, whose real name was Finn, never spoke. He was returned to his cell a battered wreck and warned he would be tortured again on the morrow if he did not name names. He had no poison pill on him but he had his shirt. With his last remaining strength he tore it into strips, knotted them together, and hanged himself.

The two deserters were *Gestapo* spies. They had been authorized by the Germans to do some sabotage at the field in order to convince the underground that they were truly anti-Nazi.

Late in November Max and a companion returned to Oslo, covering much of their Norwegian route on skis.

The outlook at Christmas was the darkest Max and his friends had ever faced. Everywhere the *Gestapo* and the Quislings were closing in.

"Something had gone wrong on the Allies' western front," Max wrote. "The tremendous steady push eastward across France, Belgium, and Holland to the Rhine had bogged down. . . . A British force was cornered in Holland and the Germans had broken through the American line in Belgium and were forcing the Yanks back, with terrible losses."

This was the desperate German counteroffensive which started in fog and snow on December 16, 1944, in the Duchy of Luxembourg and the southeastern Belgian frontier zone, know as the Battle of the Bulge.

The people of Norway were getting desperate. Virtually all joessings had agreed that if a liberating invasion did not develop soon the resistance in that country would be smashed.

"Meanwhile, week after week the *Donau* made her regular trips from Oslo to Denmark, carrying war material, troops, and prisoners," Max commented. "Time and again it was reported that British submarines or planes had sunk her. But always, and right on schedule, the huge 165-meter ship would come gliding into the harbor."

The great coup

Max's determination to get the *Donau* remained unshaken through all these tense weeks. As a companion in this job he chose Roy Nielsen, one of the gang's most daring operators, an Osloite in his middle twenties.

At Christmastime a clever plan was being hatched on the advice of a joessing who worked as an electrician at the Norwegian-American Line piers where the *Donau* regularly docked.

This worker tipped them off to the fact that there was a freight elevator at the southern end of a large warehouse on the pier which was never used. He had ascertained that when this elevator was run up a little above the level of the quay a man or even two men could slip under it when the sliding door was open. This was the only door, the elevator being merely a movable platform for goods of various types. Once the door was closed anyone under the elevator would be well hidden.

Underneath the elevator, a few feet below the floor level, was a thin steel flooring constituting the bottom part of the shaftway. The electrician told Max and his friends that he would cut a round hole in the flooring large enough for a man to drop through to the water below, partially iced over at this time of year.

A few days before Christmas, Max and Roy headed for the pier in a truck bearing two bags and a fairly large case which contained, among other things, limpets, a rope ladder, and a collapsible rubber boat. At that time there were no ships at the pier, the *Donau* being away on one of her regular runs to Denmark.

The electrician got them in the area without undue trouble, stating they had been engaged to do some special elevator repair work, pointing to their forged papers as further proof that they were experts in this type of work.

"We found the elevator slightly lifted," Max wrote. "It took only a minute, when the guard at that part of the pier had his back turned to put the stuff (which had been taken out of the truck) under it, lower the elevator to its position on a level with the pier, thus hiding our equipment, shut the door and walk away. The electrician who worked there all the time and was not under any suspicion walked along with us, and in this manner Roy and I left the pier."

After being notified that the hole had been made in the steel flooring, Roy and Max decided to return to the elevator and pump up the rubber boat so that everything would be in readiness when the *Donau* pulled in.

Having been checked in previously by the electrician, the two entered the pier area without any special difficulty. The material was still there just as they had left it, next to the newly created opening.

"We were unfolding the boat when we heard a company of men march along the pier and halt outside the elevator door," Max wrote.

"God! What was going to happen now?

"As we crouched, with our pistols ready, the men began to do their setting-up exercises. It was a detachment of the guard on duty on the pier. We went back to work with the boat. We had a small pump and it made a sound like a child's Christmas horn. When I worked it, the pump said *'Pooh! Pooh! Pooh!'* It sounded like a lot of noise under the pier and it made me nervous.

"'Give it to me,' Roy said. 'I'm more musical than you.'"

He started pumping in time with the commands the officer was barking at the guards: "Eins . . . Zwei."

"*Pooh! Pooh!*" said the pump.

"I started conducting with my hand. Roy kept time with
the pump. By the time the men broke ranks, we had the
boat full of air. We tied it up under the floor of the
pier and said a quiet prayer that no one in the patrol
boats would see it hanging there above the water. When
our friend the electrician knocked his signal on the door,
we crawled up and got away."

The importance of the *Donau* had increased markedly as
a result of the Bulge offensive. Both Max and Roy had
learned of the communiqué issued by General George
("Blood and Guts") Patton, American commander, urging
that everything possible be done to halt the movement of
German troop transports from Norway to the western front
battle zone.

These transports carried troops southward from the Finn-
ish front—fresh young troops who had become battle-wise
fighting the Russians. All these troops were equipped with
excellent winter clothing and knew how to fight in all kinds
of snow conditions, an important factor in view of the
weather prevailing at that time on the western front. The
Donau was one of the most important transportation links
in this southward flow of reinforcements.

Early in the second week of January 1945, Max and Roy
were informed by one of the joessings at the harbor that
the *Donau* had proceeded to a small harbor on Oslo Fjord
but would arrive in the capital shortly.

On January 14 they learned that a harbor official had
been instructed by the port authorities to get everything
ready for the *Donau's* arrival. The time for Roy and Max
to strike was at hand.

"I'll never forget that night [of January 14–15]," Max
remembered. "I felt as if I hadn't slept for years and yet
it was impossible to sleep. Roy and I lay in the big double
bed and time and again he would turn over and ask me
if I was asleep. I never was. We kept switching the light
on every half hour to see what time it was. Suddenly Roy
said:

" 'I'll be glad when it's all over—no matter how it turns out.' "

Both got up at 5:00 A.M. and put on their British uniforms with the Norwegian insignia "which were nice and warm."

"The uniform always had a calming effect on me. I don't know why, but that's how it was. We knew it wouldn't make it any easier for us if we were taken, but we felt more like soldiers. On top of the uniforms we wore overalls. We had made ourselves some coffee and then we said goodbye to Mrs. Maeland. She hadn't slept much herself, because she knew we were up to something very serious and, though she had no idea what it might be, our nervousness was contagious."

Then both commandos slipped quietly downstairs and strolled through the chill morning air to a nearby streetcar stop. Entering one headed for the harbor area, they reached the pier area without incident and were met by the electrician and another resistance man named Ivar, an important contact who had a steady job in the harbor.

The *Donau* was already berthed in full view at the pier, the ship and her immediate vicinity the scene of bustling activity. Any hopes of immediately proceeding to the elevator were dashed by the electrician. He informed Max and Roy that a German guard had fallen into the water and drowned. The Germans were now searching for the body in a section of the pier near the elevator and this activity might prove dangerous to the resistance plans at the moment.

"We agreed to meet at the same spot at half-past eight," Max wrote. "To fill in the time Roy and I went to the place where Karen (a young woman who had helped Max and his friends on many occasions) had her dressmaking establishment. We rolled up in rugs on the floor in the back room, turned our faces to the wall and tried to quiet our nerves."

At 8:30 A.M. they were back at the pier zone, ready for action but the electrician suggested that they wait until later in the day because there was a great deal of ice under the pier. This was too much for the two saboteurs, both tired of delays.

"I knew I couldn't take it any longer—the anxiety of waiting. I preferred to try it now. I felt a terrible nausea and suddenly vomited in the street. I started to explain that I had eaten some bad Danish eggs for breakfast. Roy just looked at me and I knew he understood. He and I set off for the gate to the pier."

Both men knew that the entire guard system was much sharper at the pier due to the fact that the *Donau* had arrived. Although their forged papers were in order and they could count on help from the electrician, Max and Roy decided on a comedy skit to avert any undue questioning by guards at the main pier gate.

Roy, who at one time had been a rather well-known heavyweight boxer, would be the star.

"He was very tall. When we reached the gate he suddenly fell on his backside—his long legs and long arms beating the air. The guards roared with laughter. For them it was a little break. Roy brushed the snow off his back and shoulders, muttering and swearing and took his toolbox that one of the Germans had picked up for him. They did not even bother to look at his papers and they merely glanced at mine.

"So we were inside the gate."

Both Max and Roy needed utmost nerve control to maintain a casual air. The Germans took no chances when the *Donau* was around. Guards at the pier had been doubled. There were thirty-five men stationed alongside the ship, armed with submachine guns, and there were guards aboard the *Donau* who had been ordered to shoot at anything they saw floating in the water that appeared the slightest bit suspicious.

"Germans, Germans, wherever we looked. All with fine white sheepskin coats over their shoulders. Where the coats were open, we could see the campaign ribbons and the iron crosses. These were the cream of the German Army . . .

"The pier was loaded with tanks, cannon and horses. 'Poor horses,' whispered Roy. All the winches were going and the cranes were working at loading the ship."

The electrician who, on this occasion, had preceded Roy and Max through the main gate was waiting for them at the elevator.

"He led us over to the door of the elevator. A guard stood by it. I asked him to move aside a little and then opened the door and jumped down. Roy followed me. We shut the door.

"We started to work right away. It was terribly cold under the pier and a north wind was blowing. But I was soaked with sweat. Suddenly there was a kick at the door. Then another. I dropped my tools and grabbed the Sten gun, ready to fire. Roy rose and peeped through the slit under the door. The face he turned toward me was full of relief.

"The troops had lined up alongside the warehouse to be out of the wind and they were kicking their heels to keep warm. We had brought along some fishing line and I used this to tie the door on the inside. We could hear every word the Germans were saying. It was about Von Rundstedt's battle of the Bulge. . . ."

In a few minutes Max and Roy heard a shouted command and could hear the Germans' footsteps receding. Then they heard the steps of one man and the door was opened a bit.

"Are you all right, Tollef [the name by which Manus was known in the resistance]?" the electrician asked.

"Yes, fine," Max answered. "Lock this door and come back in two hours."

The electrician locked the door and the two ship raiders began to get their limpets ready.

"We put the rubber boat down on the ice. Some of the air had gone out of it so we pumped it up again. There was so much noise now on the pier, we were not afraid the pump would betray us. We had taken off our overalls and were standing in British battle dress with Norwegian insignia.

"We were soldiers."

Roy and Max then loaded everything into the rubber boat. Max kicked the ice scum so that it broke and they had open water. Roy got into the boat and seized a paddle as Max continued to smash the ice layer with his boots. Both men were constantly fearful lest the ice cut a hole in the thin fabric of the boat which then and there would have doomed their operation.

"While I was breaking up an ice cake a patrol boat suddenly pulled up along the southern end of the pier. I slid into the water and kept my head up by holding on to the rubber boat, in which Roy was lying flat. I prayed they wouldn't see us or the rope ladder which he had had to leave dangling from the hole. But it was dark under the pier and we kept very silent. Presently the patrol boat went away.

"As soon as it left, I got in the rubber boat with Roy and we struggled through the lane I had broken in the ice. We came alongside the *Donau*. The limpets were ready. I produced a red crayon and wrote *With regards from King Haakon* on the first limpet . . . I put the limpet on the pole and dipped the whole length of my arm in the water as Roy paddled the rubber boat closer to the ship. Suddenly I heard a faint *ping!* as the limpet sucked on to the *Donau's* hull. I took the next limpet and fixed it; then I solemnly wrote on it *Regards from Gregers*. We put it down some seven feet from the one mentioning the King."

A total of ten limpets were affixed along the hull at various points. On every limpet Max and Roy inscribed names of various comrades who had been arrested or killed and on the last one they wrote *Regards from the Oslo Gang*. They knew that all this was something of a futile "beau geste" because writing would dissolve with any explosion but the act gave them mischievous satisfaction.

At several places the hull was so far from the pier that

the two daring paddlers feared they would be discovered
any second and riddled with bullets.

"Once we advanced too far and could look straight up
at the troops who were leaning over the *Donau's* rail. It
was 1:00 P.M. when we finished and pulled back through
the ice to the rope ladder. Very shortly after that the *Donau*
glided slowly away from her berth and out into the harbor. . . ."

The two men under the pier now perceived that another
German-operated ship, the S.S. *Rolandseck,* a 7000-ton transport, had berthed on the other side of the pier. They had
one limpet left, lying on the steel floor beneath the elevator.
Max quickly climbed up the ladder, seized the limpet, and
dropped back into the boat. Then they paddled toward the
Rolandseck.

"The ice was worse on that side of the pier and we had
to struggle a good deal to reach the ship's side by the
engine room. We gave the *Rolandseck* our last limpet."

They paddled back to the ladder and climbed up. The
boat was hauled up, deflated, and stowed in a dark corner
in the space below the elevator. After a short wait, the
electrician came and let them out, their uniforms again hidden by overalls.

"We could hear the *Donau* sounding her foghorn. . . .
We could see her out in the harbor. She was listing but
that was because she was packed with troops and they were
standing on one side, waving to those man going aboard the
Rolandseck. Roy and I waved too."

Not a single German had suspected their deadly work
and they got through the main gate after a somewhat careless check of their papers. If the guards had been more
vigilant they might have noticed something odd about their
appearance, something of which Max and Roy were fully
aware but could do nothing about. Splotches of dampness
caused by their soaked uniforms were staining their overalls
both in the upper and lower body areas.

Once outside the gate they hopped a streetcar crowded

with Norwegian workmen and a number of Germans. No one paid any attention to the two tired-looking young workmen who had apparently been engaged in arduous and damp repair work, both staring stonily through the windows.

They had barely arrived at Mrs. Maeland's apartment when Ivar came in the door after a hurried trip from the harbor. Since Mrs. Maeland was out at the time he could talk freely. Although she was loyal, details of resistance work were never divulged to her until after the war. Ivar was jubilant over their luck thus far.

The *Donau* was loaded, aside from troops, with the largest and most valuable cargo she had ever carried. From crane operators Ivar had obtained detailed information of what was aboard: 450 horses,* many motorized vehicles of various types, a considerable amount of light artillery, and large quantities of motor fuel and ammunition. Some 2000 men were aboard including 1250 men of the crack Second Mountain Regiment, ordered to proceed to the western front, 250 luftwaffe men, various groups of maintenance specialists, ship's gunners, and crew. Aboard the *Rolandseck* were 250 horses, sleighs, automobiles and motorcycles, and some 500 troops, besides the crew.

The limpets had been timed to go off after approximately nine hours, so that blast time would occur somewhere between 9:00 P.M. and 11:00 P.M. that night of January 15, 1945.

The two saboteurs thanked Ivar for this encouraging news before he left, then ate some food, shed their wet uniforms and overalls and went to bed, falling asleep at once.

Early next morning Max and Roy, in civilian clothes, headed for the vicinity of the pier. Their faces fell. There was the *Rolandseck* in her berth. Nothing had happened. Disconsolately Max and Roy returned to their apartment.

---

* The Germans used horses extensively to haul supplies during World War II. The animals were particularly valuable to them at this time due to gasoline shortages.

Mrs. Maeland was there and was shocked by their haggard looks and immediately brewed them some strong coffee.

Then the phone jangled. Max picked it up and uttered a cautious "Hello, who is it?"

A man's voice answered, its tone revealing jubilance. "It's me, Ivar. Everything's perfect."

"What are you saying?" Max asked tensely. "Has anything happened?"

"Plenty!" Ivar replied with a laugh. "Meet me at the same place as yesterday in half an hour."

Then he hung up and Max, hanging up his receiver, signaled to Roy and both hurriedly left the apartment. The news they got from Ivar in a secluded spot was very good.

The *Donau* was finished.

The ship was reaching the end of Oslo Fjord, about eighty miles long, and was about to head for the open sea when the explosions had started with terrifying effect.

The captain, in a desperate maneuver, had immediately sailed her full speed to the nearby shore and had managed to run her bow on land before she sank at the stern, water pouring over most of the ship.

"The horses and all the material were now under water," Max learned from Ivar. "Two hundred ambulances and Red cross automobiles had been driven down from Oslo to take care of the injured. The mate of the *Donau* had managed to get ashore and had phoned Oslo to report sabotage on his ship and recommend that the *Rolandseck* be examined. The pier had been barred and all the troops had been taken off while they looked over her. But they found nothing. The troops went aboard again and the loading of the cargo went on. Just as they were about to pull out from the pier, the limpet exploded, making a hole more than a meter and a half in diameter and almost three meters below water level. The *Rolandseck* was sinking at the pier. She wouldn't be easy to repair, for all the electrical equipment was damaged by water which poured into the gaping hole."

The Germans never disclosed how many casualties had

occurred aboard the *Donau* but it was learned later that
at least a thousand Germans had either been killed or
wounded by the blasts or had drowned.

Although this feat marked the end of Max's and Roy's
operations against shipping, their activities in the underground continued. The final phases of the resistance in Norway were the worst Max ever endured. It was cut to pieces
in raid after raid even though Allied victory was closer than
ever. One of the gang's most trusted men, named Olav,
was shot and killed by the *Gestapo* in an apartment am-
bush. Within half an hour Roy entered the same apartment.
Germans materialized, firing from the hip. Roy made a
desperate attempt to escape up a flight of stairs but was
mowed down and died where he fell.

Max and some friends were in Stockholm for a brief visit
to confer on new measures against the Nazis when the news
came in May that Germany had finally capitulated. Dread
Adolf was dead, a suicide in Berlin, and sawdust Caesar
Mussolini had been executed by Italian patriots.

Amid the general jubilation, Max and some of his friends
returned to Oslo, openly wearing their British battle uniforms. For some time everybody thought they were the
advance guard of British forces which they believed had arrived in Norway, and cheered them frantically, somewhat
to the arrivals' amusement. In the subsequent return of King
Haakon and Crown Prince Olaf to Norway, Max and other
members of the Oslo gang were designated bodyguards to
the royal family because of the lurking danger of an attempted assassination by some die-hard Nazi.

It was a very tense time for Max. He sat in the royal
car alongside the chauffeur—also a member of the gang.
Max, armed with a tommy gun, had orders to throw himself on any explosive which might be hurled into the car
and constantly scan crowds, roofs, and windows. Fortunately, nothing happened.

Max and his fiancée were married in 1945 after she had
been introduced to his father and mother in separate visits.

Many high decorations were bestowed on Max for his wartime feats—among the most daring in the entire underground war. Becoming a successful businessman in Norway after the war, he lives there today, one of the country's national heroes. He received the Distinguished Service Cross from the United States and the Distinguished Service Order and Military Cross with Bar from Britain.

The first meeting between Max, his fiancée, and his father had a humorous twist.

"We went up into the country, beyond Bergen, to a little village. It was in the mountain towering above it that my father lived his hermit life with his books, his dog and his gun. I had written him that we were coming and so he came down from the mountain and was waiting at the village inn when we drove up.

"After an exchange of greetings he looked me straight in the eye.

" 'Well, Max, how many Germans did you kill?'

" 'I don't know,' I said. 'A few anyway.'

" 'Humph!' He came over to the car to look at the luggage we had brought. 'Did you bring a fishing rod?'

" 'No!'

" 'Well, I have one I can let you use. We'll go out and get a salmon.'

"And then I was really sure the war was over."

5

Luxembourg, Holland, Belgium

When the Hun is poor and down
He's the humblest man in town
But once he climbs and holds the rod
He smites his fellowmen—and God!

A verse by the seventeenth-century
Dutch poet, Jakob Cats

PSYCHOLOGICAL WARFARE

On a balmy summer Sunday of 1941 the Nazi *Ortsgruppenleiter* in the village of Rumelange awakened late in the morning from a deep sleep abetted by large doses of wine and cognac he had downed the previous evening.

The German was the Nazi administrator of the village, ensconced in a valley in the tiny Duchy of Luxembourg, sandwiched between Germany, France, and Belgium. A gross man with beady eyes, hated by all his subjects, he occupied at that time a floor in one of the better buildings in the village, rent free. After various grunts and yawns, the German rose from his bed and tucking his feet into slippers, still in his pajamas, headed for the apartment door, ponderously and somewhat unsteadily. Enroute to the bathroom outside, he opened the door and almost immediately uttered some unprintable German oaths.

One of the hilarious hunts of the resistance annals was about to occur in Rumelange. It was typical of the many ingenious jokes carried out by the Luxembourgers to prickle the Germans and pro-Nazis and complement more violent forms of resistance following the seizure of the duchy in May 1940.

Persons unknown had been active in the building—with paint pots—while the German snored the night hours away.

The German's eyes bulged with anger the moment he saw what had been done to the staircase leading downstairs from the landing in front of his bedroom. The upper banisters and steps had been freshly painted red, white, and blue, the colors linked with the Allies during the war.

Whoever had done the job had been careless. Obviously their paint pots had leaked, for telltale spots of paint were visible on the lower steps and in the main hallway leading to the front door of the house.

The malefactors had left a trail! Promptly the German paddled down the stairs and stormed through the front door into the sunlight. Here were more splotches of paint on the ground and he followed them as fast as he could. Round one corner, then another, the hunter trotted, then straight through the building's garden, to a stone wall overlooking a road. The splashes of paint on the ground ended here. At the base of the wall, neatly aligned, were three half-empty cans containing the red, white, and blue pigments. A big red "V"—the popular "V for Victory" symbol of all anti-Nazis—adorned the wall above the cans.

The men who had done the painting and other residents witnessed most of the skit from nearby windows or suitable hiding places in the vicinity. No one was ever caught.

This was only one of various methods of using colors to irritate the tyrants. In Rumelange and other villages the Luxembourgers repeatedly painted chickens with splashes of red, white, and blue, It proved exhilarating to see the Germans and their pro-Nazi friends—of which there were very few in Luxembourg—chase these "patriotic" fowls in yards and alleyways.

On another occasion the Rumelangers staged something more spectacular. On a wintry day the Germans suddenly beheld a flag waving proudly from the top of a 150-foot-high factory chimney. It was the red, yellow, and black banner of Luxembourg. An angry German sergeant rushed forward and began to climb the outside of the chimney by the iron rungs set there for the purpose, believing he would haul down the flag without difficulty.

He was disillusioned, however, when he reached a point only six feet from the chimney's summit. Here the rungs ended. The flag-hoister had foresightedly removed them on his way down. The Nazis brought the flag down later in the day—after firing several hundred rounds of machine-gun bullets.

In spite of occasional humorous incidents like these the struggle against the Germans in Luxembourg—the tiniest land seized by Hitler—was just as grim as in other conquered countries. Considering the number of its inhabitants, some 300,000 persons, it was outstanding.

There was no question of any armed defense when the Germans poured in on May 10, 1940. The duchy's army— if it can be called that—never exceeded some 400 volunteers, a minuscule force, lacking planes, tanks, or heavy artillery.

Grand Duchess Charlotte, the beloved ruler of the beautiful country, members of her family and government, fled the country when the Germans came. Very wisely, the Luxembourg government had taken measures before 1939 providing for such action in case of invasion. As a result the people were fully aware that such a move was absolutely necessary to ensure continued functioning of a legal, unfettered government abroad.

Proceeding through France on a trip which would terminate in England, the Grand Duchess and members of her government formally issued a declaration of war on Germany, certainly a case of David challenging Goliath.

Throughout the occupation—which ended in the fall of 1944 when American troops arrived—the Luxembourgers clashed repeatedly with the Nazi overlords. The latter had arbitrarily proclaimed the land a district of the Reich itself. Thousands of men and women were conscripted for forced labor or risked imprisonment, torture, and death for espionage, aiding the escapes of Allied soldiers and airmen, distribution of illegal newspapers and sabotage of various types. A predominantly Catholic country, priests, nuns, and monks suffered extremely harsh treatment, including imprisonment and in some cases death. Completely surrounded by large German-held areas, escape from Luxembourg was more difficult than from other countries. Various resistance groups struggled courageously to help the Jews in the Duchy but the chance of effecting mass escapes was nil. Of the four thousand Jews in Luxembourg on May 10, three thousand perished in concentration camps.

According to Ronald Seth in his well-authenticated book, *The Undaunted*, a history of resistance in World War II, the first truly important tip-off on German flying bomb experiments reached London from Luxembourg.*

Claiming that Luxembourg was part of the Reich, Gustave Simon, the Nazi plenipotentiary, a diseased sadist nicknamed the Dwarf of Triers, forced some 12,000 young Luxembourgers to enroll in the German armed forces. One of these was assigned as guard to some strange underground installations in Peenemünde, the island in the Baltic used by the Germans for flying bomb research.

Returning to Luxembourg on leave, he gave an accurate description of the installations to Edmond Goergen, a noted Luxembourg artist. At the time Goergen worked at the big Luxembourg radio station. Secretly he was busy funneling anti-Nazi intelligence out of the country. Although he had no clue to its full importance, he succeeded in conveying the information in full to London.

An outstanding example of courage was shown by four young Luxembourgers in a minor but desperate fray in Heinerscheid forest. The four were hiding in a disused bunker where for several days they sheltered two American airmen who had been shot down. When the Americans left for another point on instructions from resistance leaders, two

---

* These were the V-1's ("buzz bombs") and V-2's used largely against London. The letter V used to designate these rocket missiles meant they were Vergeltungswaffen (vengeance weapons).

hundred German soldiers closed in on the bunker. The young patriots had only one revolver and half a dozen rounds of ammunition between them but they defied German orders to surrender.

One of the German troopers then crawled toward the encircled bunker to throw in a grenade. One of the besieged men killed him and another dashed out, seized the dead man's fast-firing Schmeisser pistol and his ammunition, and re-entered the bunker, miraculously untouched in spite of heavy enemy fire.

The Luxembourgers fought till all ammunition was exhausted. When the Germans entered the bunker the defenders were still there—all four lying dead on the ground.

DUTCH TREAT

The people of Holland and Belgium, whose countries also were pounced upon by Hitler on May 10, 1940, similarly wrote stirring chapters in the secret war.

Revered Queen Wilhelmina, Crown Princess Juliana, the present Dutch sovereign, and her husband, Prince Bernhard, had to flee the country almost immediately so that a legitimate government-in-exile could be established in Britain.

The small Dutch army fought bravely against sweeping air-land assaults but had to surrender in five days. During the invasion Holland was the first nation in the west to feel the full weight of Hitler's air power. Luftwaffe planes mercilessly bombed the big city of Rotterdam, killing and wounding thousands, one of the most inexcusable terror attacks of the entire war. The attack served no military purpose whatsoever but it proved a constant spur to Dutch anger in the protracted underground struggle ahead.

At first the Dutch were deeply shaken by the departure of Wilhelmina but they soon realized that it was an imperative and wise move. Aside from preventing Nazi detention of the Queen, it ensured a continuation of the fight outside conquered territory and pro-Allied administration of

Holland's overseas territories, including the vast East Indies. Throughout the occupation all Hollanders—Dutch pro-Nazis excepted—remained unswervingly loyal to the royal ruling house, the House of Orange.

Suitably enough, Holland, a land famous for its flowers, was the scene of the biggest floral anti-Nazi demonstration of the war.

The first big anti-Nazi demonstration occurred on Sunday, June 30, 1940. Confronted with German edicts forbidding the wearing of orange flowers or any orange colored symbols, huge throngs of Hollanders appeared on the streets of cities, towns, and villages that sunny day wearing white carnations.

The Germans and the Dutch Nazis, whose fuehrer was pudgy Anton Otto Mussert, had failed to ban carnations. The day previous, June 29, was the birthday of Prince Bernhard, who was very popular with the Dutch. A white carnation was his favorite flower.

Huge bouquets of carnations and other flowers were placed on the steps of the Royal Palace in The Hague and at the bases of statues of historic Dutch personages.

It was not until late in the day that the full significance of this Sunday activity dawned on Germans and their pro-Nazi hirelings. Almost immediately bands of armed Dutch Nazis began roaming through the streets tearing the flowers from the buttonholes of strollers.

Violent disorders occurred throughout the country and before the day was over carnations drew blood. When night fell Dutch longshoremen, sailors, truck drivers, and more daring teen-age students gathered in taverns and at street corners and defied any Nazis they saw to rip off the carnations they were wearing. In many instances the Nazis did succeed in grasping the flowers but they suffered terrible cuts. Razor blades had been concealed in the flowers.

Dutch tempers were further inflamed when the Germans began repressive action against Holland's 120,000 Jews in October, much sooner than they did in Denmark, Norway, or Luxembourg. German attempts to convince the Hollanders that the Jews were subhumans meriting such action failed completely. Men and women helped the Jews in every possible fashion, often suffering imprisonment or death as a result. The girl whose name eventually would be known throughout the world was one of the many Jewish persons for whom the Dutch risked their freedom and their lives. She was little Anne Frank with the pretty, pensive face who faithfully kept a diary while in hiding in Holland and later perished in a concentration camp. When her story was told in book form and dramatized for the stage after the war it profoundly stirred people in all countries, including Germans.

Young boys were among the most daring resistants. Shortly after the invasion six teen-age schoolboys of Haarlem organized a secret sabotage ring somewhat similar to the Churchill Club in Aalborg, Denmark. The ring had various departments to cover different types of sabotage such as electrical, chemical, and incendiary operations. They caused some damage to military and civil equipment before three of them were caught while attempting to cut a German telephone cable. The three others were also caught and all six sentenced to three years' imprisonment in Haarlem by a German Military Court.

The Protestant and Catholic clergy maintained an adamant stand against Germans and the Dutch Nazis, scoring their anti-Jewish and other repressive measures in ringing words from the pulpit and in pastoral letters. Catholic bishops, wielding a powerful religious weapon, ruled that it was a mortal sin to belong to the pro-Nazi party of Mussert and forbade the granting of Sacraments to any of its members. This ruling was stoutly upheld by Catholic clerics time and again in spite of harsh, but somewhat futile counteraction by the traitors and their German masters.

Widespread strikes by factory workers, longshoremen and other shipping workers, and railwaymen harried the Germans repeatedly, notably in February 1941 and in the spring of 1943. Frequently, such action triggered violent clashes accompanied by bloodshed and the shooting of numerous hostages. These strikes, which were part of the general resistance movement, were complemented by intensive distribution of illegal newspapers and secret sabotage strikes against munitions and other plants serving the Germans.

Dutch saboteurs were unquestionably involved in the mysterious disappearance of a submarine constructed under German supervision at Schiedam. When the brand-new craft, thoroughly checked by the Germans and having a German crew aboard, slid down the ways at Schiedam, near Rotterdam, she sank like a stone in deep water, disappearing forever. The Germans never were able to convict anyone of sabotage in this occurrence.

The Dutch waged a particularly clever jestkrieg against the Nazis, which in spite of its humorous overtones was dangerous in every instance.

One Hollander got so angry over the German rationing of clothes and general economic plundering that he resorted to a particularly original form of protest. It would have given the vapors to any respectable Victorian lady if such a person had been present.

He strolled out into the streets of a big city, reportedly Amsterdam, on a blustery day. He was naked except for shoes, socks, and hat, carrying an opened umbrella above his head. A bystander who happened to have a camera on him took a snapshot of the man from the rear and smuggled it out of the country. It was eventually published in a big American magazine and elsewhere. The Germans immediately seized the man and sped him to a concentration camp. As far as is known this Hollander—who had a special kind of courage—survived the war but his name is lost to history.

In Vlissingen (Flushing) a Dutch boy of ten, who had a smattering of the German language, gave a strolling German officer a notable verbal knockout.

The German came up to the boy and in a somewhat haughty manner asked him to identify a nearby statue.

This boy had an affliction. He stuttered badly. His reply was:

"Th-th-that i-i-is our a-a-a-Admiral d-d-de Ruyter, who defeated the b-b-b-British."

This was a reference to Holland's most famous seaman who successfully battled the English in past centuries, the statue his likeness.

The officer frowned and mimicking the boy said: "S-s-so, th-th-that is o-o-old de Ruyter, j-u-u-st t-th-think of that."

He received a fast answer: "D-d-d-don't imitate m-m-me, imitate him."

With this retort, the boy vanished round the corner of a nearby building.

Holland gin is a famous drink throughout the world, more potent, more of a concentrated liqueur than the alcoholic beverage of that name popular in this country. In Schiedam, where the world-famous draught is bottled and poured into distinctive clay jars, a German soldier met with a somewhat traumatic experience.

On a cold night he was accosted by some seemingly friendly young Hollanders. Like all Germans in Holland he had received a full dose of the cold shoulder for weeks. He was quite happy when they invited him to come to an apartment nearby where one of them lived.

Once in the apartment, Schiedam gin began to flow freely, particularly in the German's direction, and everything was *gemuetlich* with the Hollanders loud in their praise of Hitler, German *kultur* and the New Order.

Finally the Hollanders smilingly bade their friend farewell and sent him, staggering but happy, downstairs, urging him to return to his headquarters. After weaving through the night-cloaked streets, the German soldier arrived at his destination and reported to his superior officer. He raised his arm in a vague "Heil Hitler!" salute and with a somewhat incoherent excuse for his lateness turned and headed for his nearby barracks. A shout from the officer stopped him dead in his tracks.

His friends had put a big orange placard on his back, of which he was totally unaware. On the placard in black were written in German the words:

"Even though I am a Hitler dog, I bear the color orange on my posterior."

THE EARTH-SHAKING BLAST

The neighboring Belgians fought with particular gallantry in May to stem the German juggernaut but their armed resistance was as futile as that of other countries.

This country was confronted almost immediately with a problem which would not be solved until some five years after the war. Late in May, King Leopold capitulated suddenly, rejecting the urgings of his ministers to flee the country and set up a Belgian government in London. His action angered many persons in Belgium as well as Allied leaders, creating one of the most bitter controversies of the war. He and members of the royal family remained virtual prisoners of the Germans for the duration, first at Laeken Castle in Belgium and after the Allied invasion of 1944 in Germany and Austria. During this time a Belgian government-in-exile formed by various Belgian statesmen functioned in London.

The King, who resided in Switzerland after the Allied victory in May 1945, went back to Belgium in 1950 after a national plebiscite on this issue. Only 57 per cent of the voters approved his return. He was soon obliged to abdicate in favor of his son, Prince Baudouin, who is the present ruler.

This troublesome development—which largely prevented the King from serving as an inspiration to his people during many dark years—did not crush Belgium's combative spirit. The resistance in this country was as heroic as in any other land, its casualties among resistants of both sexes extremely heavy.

At Tessenderloo there was a big chemical plant controlled by the Germans specializing in the manufacture of nitrate of ammonia, which has tremendous explosive power.

A vast and deep concrete vat had been built in the plant where the factory's daily output was stored. Elaborate precautions against fire had been taken by the Germans. The slightest spark in such a plant, especially in or near the vat, spelled doom.

Members of the heroic White Brigade, one of Belgium's outstanding underground formations, decided that somehow the plant would have to be blasted. The decision was a terrible one to make because they knew that such action would be the death of many innocent Belgians. On the other hand its destruction would undoubtedly prevent the death of hundreds of thousands of Allied soldiers.

All realized that any attempts to cause an explosion from a distance with a plunger and electric wires were futile from the start in this instance. The German watch was close. Someone had to volunteer to touch off a spark, knowing he would die in the act. A Flemish worker at the plant reportedly volunteered for the task which could have only one end, although what hero was involved and what his name was is not known to this day.

When asked if he was really determined to do so, this Belgian assertedly recalled the example of the workers in the big Czech Skoda works. In sabotaging their plant rather than let it function for the Germans, these men had died in a boiling river of molten metal.

"What a Czech can do a Belgian can too," the Flemish worker stated.

On the morning of April 29, 1942, he entered the plant.

That morning the sky was clear, the "air as warm as on that day almost two years before when the Germans had marched in," Robert Goffin writes in his thrilling account of various phases of Belgian resistance in the book *The*

White Brigade. Peasants worked in their fields amid the budding flowers. And then the world was engulfed in an awful nothingness.

"The sound of the explosion was so tremendous that many did not hear it. Only their eyes recorded the chaos, soon yielding to a kind of instinctive perception. For miles around houses were unroofed and shattered and the sky was black as legend tells us it was at the hour of the Crucifixion. The product of years of labor and finance and scheming was restored in a split second to its primordial dust."

Tessenderloo itself had simply been wiped out.

"Nothing remained of its houses, its school, its inn and little of its inhabitants," Goffin writes. "More than 250 of them had been killed outright."

The injured in the Tessenderloo area totaled some 2100 persons. In subsequent days many of these succumbed to their injuries.

A rescue worker "who was among the dozens called to the scene said later that in a radius of nearly ten miles there was not a whole window, not a tree firm and straight." The newspaper, *Independent Belgium,* published in England reported:

"Nothing remained of the factory save the stumps of the chimneys and a vast crater surrounded by smaller ones. Great masses of steel and concrete had been shot into the air to fall and flatten buildings or bury themselves in the ground.

"In the great crater in the center of the plant, dirty liquid of unknown origin floated below its edges, covered with a greenish oil-like substance. Farther away there was a mass of twisted rails. In all the ruins it was often necessary to use dynamite before bodies could be removed."

In this hecatomb one of the anti-Nazi underground's unknown soldiers fulfilled an assignment—his deed another bright thread in a tapestry of valor spun by so many in the secret conflict which silently, savagely, anonymously helped topple the pillars of Nazidom and Fascism.

EPILOGUE

For 'tis the sport to have the engineer
Hoist with his own petar.

From Hamlet by William Shakespeare

And when the pillars cracked and tumbled, the man with the receding chin wandered fearfully through Armageddon's dust, a black patch over one eye and his uniform that of a German rural policeman.

The Nemesis of the resistance himself had gone underground. His mustache shaved off, he was heading for his native Bavaria when he was seized at a British road control point between Hamburg and Bremerhaven in northern Germany on May 21.

"Private" Heinrich Himmler was stripped and searched and forced to don a British private's uniform since poison might be hidden in his German garb.

But the search was not thorough enough.

When a medical officer was summoned to effect a more thorough search of his person Himmler suddenly ground his teeth on a cyanide pill he had kept hidden in his mouth. The one-time terror overlord, the former chicken farmer with icy eyes, reeled and collapsed. He was dead in 12 minutes.

Fate had even denied him the honor of dying in a German uniform.

Sic semper tyrannis! (Thus ever to all tyrants).

BIBLIOGRAPHY
(A partial listing of sources consulted for this book)

France

Ten Thousand Eyes by Richard Collier, E. P. Dutton & Co., 1958.

Histoire de la Résistance by Henri Michel, Presses Universitaires de France, 1950.

Vercors, Citadelle de la Résistance by Captain Lemoin, Fernand Nathan.

Sabotage et Guerrilla by Pierre de Preval, Berger-Levrault.

And There Was Light by Jacques Lusseyran, Little, Brown and Company, 1963.

The Unknown Warriors by Guillain de Bénouville, Simon and Schuster, 1949.

The Republic of Silence by A. J. Liebling, Harcourt, Brace & Co., 1947.

Paris Underground by Etta Shiber in collaboration with Anne and Paul Dupré, Charles Scribner's Sons, 1943.

The Courage of Fear by Roxane Pitt, Duell, Sloan & Pearce, Inc., 1957.

An Army of Amateurs by Philippe de Vomécourt, Doubleday and Co., 1961.

Tartan Pimpernel by Donald Caskie, Oldbourne (London), 1957.

Duel of Wits by Peter Churchill, G. P. Putnam's Sons, 1953.

An Army of Shadows by Joseph Kessel, Alfred A. Knopf, Inc., 1944.

Ten Steps to Hope by Col. Rémy, first published in France by Presses de la Cité in 1959 and by Arthur Barker, Ltd., London, 1960.

Denmark

The Savage Canary by David Lampe, Cassell and Company, 1957, London, Ballantine Books, New York, 1960, under the title *The Danish Resistance.*

Rescue in Denmark by Harold Flender, Simon and Schuster, 1963.

The Undaunted by Ronald Seth, Philosophical Library, Inc., 1956.

Denmark by Karin Michaelis in the book *The Sixth Column*, Alliance Book Corporation, New York, 1942.

Norway

Norway, Her Invasion and Occupation, by Amanda Johnson, Bowen Press, Decatur, Ga., 1948.

Norway by Tor Myklebost and Theodore Broch in the book *The Sixth Column.*

Nine Lives Before Thirty by Max Manus in collaboration with Dorothy Giles, Doubleday and Co., 1947.

Young Patriots by Hester O'Neill, Thomas Nelson & Sons, London, 1948.

Skis against the Atom by Knut Haukelid, Wm. Kimber, London, 1954.

The Gestapo at Work in Norway, an official publication of the Norwegian government.

Blood on the Midnight Sun by Hans Christian Adamson and Per Klem, W. W. Norton and Co., 1964.

Luxembourg, Holland, Belgium

Geschichte Luxemburgs im Zweiter Weltkrieg by Paul Weber, Victor Buck, Luxembourg.

Quatre Années de Lutte by A. Rodesch, Ney-Eicher, Luxembourg, 1947.

Luxembourg by Ronald Seth in his book *The Undaunted.*

Patrouille Phantome by Victor Eloy, Pascal and Co., Brussels.

The White Brigade by Robert Goffin, Doubleday and Co., 1944.

Le Passage de l'Iratay by William Ugeux, Henneuse and Co., Lyon, France, 1962.

London Calling North Pole by H. J. Giskes, British Book Centre
and Wm. Kimber, 1953.
The Silent War by Allard Martens and Daphne Dunlop, Hodder
and Stoughton, London, 1961.
Holland Fights the Nazis by L. De Jong, Lindsay Drummond
and Co., London, 1942.

General

The Rise and Fall of the Third Reich by William Shirer, Simon
and Schuster, 1960.
The Scourge of the Swastika by Lord Russell, Philosophical
Library, 1954, and Ballantine Books, seventh printing, 1961.
Gestapo by Edward Crankshaw, The Viking Press, 1956, and
Pyramid Publications, Inc., 1961.

Note: The researcher also will be guided to vast amounts of material in an index card drawer entitled "Patriotic and Resistance Movements, World War II" on the 3rd floor of the New York Public Library at 42nd St. and Fifth Avenue.